THE ICON EFFECT

HOW THE RIGHT MENTOR CAN CHANGE THE COURSE OF YOUR LIFE, FOREVER.

By Darren Sugiyama

www.DarrenSugiyama.com

Copyright © 2012 Darren Sugiyama
ISBN: 978-0-9892619-0-6

This book is dedicated to everyone that has the guts to dream big. This is *my* story. This is *your* story. This is *our* story.

DARREN SUGIYAMA

Table Of Contents

Chapter One
My First Encounter With The Icon

It was 5:03 a.m. and my alarm clock was set to go off in 57 minutes. I was exhausted and wired at the same time, which didn't seem possible, but having my wife leave me didn't seem possible either.

My mind was racing.

I barely got any sleep that night, tossing and turning, nightmare after nightmare.

Sometimes, I wished I could retreat back into my nightmares because they were far less painful than my actual life.

My therapist told me that the pain in my heart would decrease over time, but the knot in my stomach seemed to grow bigger as the days went on.

What did I do to deserve this?

I gave her everything I had, but apparently, that wasn't good enough.

I thought I was a good person. I went to church. I had a degree – three degrees, in fact.

I didn't think I was terribly ugly.

So why'd she leave me?

There was a time that she loved me enough to marry me. I just couldn't seem to figure out where things went wrong.

Maybe I didn't make enough money. I knew there were a lot of *rich guys* out there. Maybe she wanted to be with one of them.

Maybe I neglected her. I must admit, I thought about my career a lot more than I used to, but that was only to become a better provider for her.

I didn't have much to show for my new money-making efforts, and so maybe she lost faith in me, watching me fail so many times, over and over.

I probably over-promised in my attempts to impress her with my fabricated bright future, and becoming successful was taking a lot longer than I expected.

I remember telling her when we first got married, "Honey, I'm gonna make us rich! I'm gonna buy us a mansion in Beverly Hills... you're gonna retire early... and we'll travel the world, first class!"

"Vincent, you've got to be more *realistic*," she'd say.

"What are you talking about? I don't want to be realistic! I want to be rich! I want to be able to give you the best!" I'd emphatically retort.

My rants of grandeur would get her hopes up temporarily, but over time, as I had nothing to show for my entrepreneurial efforts, she became emotionally callous to my verbal aspirations.

"I'll believe it when I see it," she'd say.

Her little jabs at my dreams would chip away at my confidence, and each little jab took away a piece of my manhood. They would be constant little reminders that I had not yet become the man I truly wanted to be.

And this, perhaps, is every man's greatest fear – the fear that we might find out who we *really* are – and that who we really are is not who we *want* to be.

"Why can't you just get excited with me? That's part of the fun of having big dreams! Don't you want to dream?" I'd accusatorily ask in my most painstakingly frustrated tone of voice.

"I'm just tired of you getting my hopes up, Vincent. I'm tired of being disappointed. You should have just kept your job as a teacher. You could have had tenure by now, and we could have been living comfortably. We could have saved up and bought a house by now. But here we are, barely making rent in this tiny little apartment, and you keep talking about how rich we're going to be. It's exhausting, Vincent – this emotional rollercoaster. You keep coming home all excited about some sort of new business opportunity, and they all end up the same, going nowhere. I don't know why you had to quit your job. You had a *good* job."

Sure it was devastating every time one of my business opportunities didn't pan out, but somehow, I had the ability to get back up after I got knocked down and take another big swing, always swinging for the fences.

I wanted to hit the big time.

I wanted to hit homeruns, even if that meant striking out on occasion.

But the reality was that I wasn't striking out on *occasion*.

All I was doing was striking out, and after getting knocked down so many times, she just couldn't seem to get back up with the same vigor that I was able to.

I vividly remember one Sunday afternoon, she came home from the gym as I was sitting on the couch in our living room, answering emails.

As she entered the living room, I could hear the friction between the soles of her shoes and the carpet. She slowly came to a stop, standing there in silence, staring at the floor.

It was an excruciatingly *loud* silence.

As she uneasily shifted her weight back and forth between her feet, I could sense her heart rate rapidly and irregularly increasing as she let out a very awkward sigh.

"Vincent, we need to talk."

I kept working... *hearing*, but not really *listening*.

"Vincent. I've given this a lot of thought over the last few weeks, and I've made up my mind, so please don't try to talk me out of it."

I put my laptop computer down and sat up, looking at her with perturbed irritation.

"Vincent, I don't want to be married to you anymore."

"What... what do you mean?"

"Look Vincent, I can't do this anymore. I can't live like this. I'm tired of worrying about making next month's rent. I'm tired of just barely getting by every month. I can't take it. You're always telling me…"

"Wait a minute!" I argumentatively snapped. "I thought we were in this together! I thought we talked about this! No one gets rich overnight! Stuff like this takes time, and I've got this deal I'm working on, and it's really coming together. I'm really close to…"

"That's just it Vincent! You've always got some *deal* you're working on, and it's always some pie-in-the-sky get-rich-quick scheme, and…"

"What do you want me to do? Quit? Give up on my dream and go back to my old crappy job? I can't do that! I *won't* do that! I will *never* do that!"

"Vincent, it's…"

"Look, we can go to marriage counseling. I won't give up on my dream, and I won't give up on our marriage either. Whatever needs to be done – whatever changes I need to make – we can get through this. Tomorrow morning, I'll call Pastor Keith. I'll find out when he can see us and…"

"Vincent," she paused. "It's… it's over."

"No! Don't say that! We can…"

"Vincent, stop! I've already made up my mind and…"

"It's NOT over! We can make it work!" I desperately yelled at the top of my lungs.

"Please! I'll do anything you want," I pleaded.

I scrambled for the right words.

I could feel each drop of warm sweat seeping out of my pores. My heart was pounding through my chest, and without consciously thinking through it, I blurted out my last plea in desperation.

"Okay, I'll quit my business!"

I couldn't believe those words left my lips.

There was a deafening silence that overcame the room with my exclamation of surrender.

It was as if all sound had been immediately sucked into a giant vacuum, and the world stopped spinning on its axis.

I slowly stood up in a painfully uncomfortable posture – hands clasped tightly behind my neck – with every ounce of effort trying not to unravel in front of her.

And in a soft, defeated voice, I repeated those words that absolutely killed me to say.

"I'll... I'll quit my business."

"Wh-what?" she stuttered in unmitigated disbelief.

"I said I'll quit, okay? If... if that's what you want... I'll quit. If that will save our marriage, I'll quit and go back to my old job."

There was another long, awkward moment of silence that felt like it lasted a millennium.

Then I softly uttered, "Please don't leave me. Please."

"But you hated your old job."

"I hate divorce more," I said, which was followed by another long, silent pause, as I uneasily exhaled in staccato.

"Vincent, it's too late."

"Is there another guy? Did you meet someone else?"

"No," she unconvincingly said, dismissing my accusatory question.

By the look on her face, and her overt attempt to avoid eye contact with me, I could tell she was lying.

"Honey, give me another chance! Please!" I pleaded.

She just stared across the room, looking right past me, as if I didn't exist.

"Please, just give me one more..."

"Vincent... it's over," she said, interrupting me in a faint, distracted whisper of a voice.

I interjected, "Please! Just one more chance. I'll…"

"Vincent!" she exclaimed with finality.

As her gaze past me turned into a deep stare into my soul, her eyes looked at me with pity. And as a man, there's nothing worse than to be looked upon with pity… especially by a woman.

It's emasculating.

I would have much preferred to be yelled at, because in a strange way, being yelled at is far easier on the heart and the ego.

At least in a yelling match, you can yell back, defending yourself. But when a woman looks at you with pity – well, as she said – it's over.

It had been seven months since she left.

All I know is that I woke up everyday feeling like a failure.

As I laid in bed obsessing about what happened – as I did every morning – my 57 minutes were up and my alarm clock went off.

It was time for me to start another lack-luster day.

I peeled myself out of bed and walked into the bathroom of my studio apartment like a zombie, and as I stared at myself in the mirror, I did in fact look like the walking dead.

My morning ritual consisted of brushing my teeth in slow motion, showering with my stress-reducing aromatherapy body wash that obviously wasn't working very well, and then listening to my motivational audio program in my car as I drove to my sales appointments.

I had three degrees, including a Master's Degree, but I was only making $29,500 per year at my old teaching job, and my co-workers were a bunch of complacent conformists that didn't have any aspirations to achieve greatness.

The majority of my teaching counterparts hated what they did for a living too, but they didn't have the guts to admit it.

However, a select few of them *loved* teaching, and typically, those were the ones that were really great teachers.

I'd like to think that I started off that way.

I actually really enjoyed working with my students. I just grew to detest the bureaucratic nonsense, inept administrators, and the complacency of many of the other teachers. It made me sick to my stomach.

Only 10% of the time was I able to really talk to my students about what I thought was important, and over 90% of my time was spent administratively administrating.

Most of my time was spent carrying out the required curriculum, which I thought was garbage. It got to the point to where I felt like a hypocrite, teaching my students to memorize and regurgitate irrelevant information that I knew they'd never use in life.

So I quit my teaching job and started my own business, a decision my ex-wife absolutely hated, and in her infinite *wisdumb*, she convinced me to shut it down after just six months.

She witnessed me start new venture after new venture, and after a series of six business ventures that all ended up flopping, there I was, starting my seventh.

Essentially, I was an independent sales rep for a vitamin company, which basically meant that I was on straight-commission, with no benefits, and as my father constantly reminded me every time I talked to him, I was dead broke.

I had set up a deal with a chiropractor and a physical therapist where they would refer their patients to me, and I'd set them up on nutritional supplement programs.

The problem was, I wasn't getting as many patient referrals as I used to, and my dismal business was becoming more and more dismal.

I was driving an economy car with decent gas mileage, I lived paycheck to paycheck, and when I read my favorite magazine, *Architectural Digest*, I'd get even more depressed because I knew that with the way my career was going, there was no way I was ever going to be able to afford even a modest house, let alone a mansion like the ones in the magazine.

So there I was.

26-years old.

Divorced.

And alone.

This was *not* how I thought my life was going to turn out.

I remembered back in college, I laughed a lot more. I had tons of friends and got invited to tons of parties... parties where I was the life of the party, or so I thought.

I was happy.

So what the heck happened?

My life had become pitiful and depressing.

The only thing that put a smile on my face was surfing. It was the one escape I had where in that exhilarating moment of riding a wave, all of my problems seemed nonexistent.

There was no one judging me.

It was just me and the waves.

Part of the joy of surfing is the exhilarating feeling of riding the wave. Part of it is just being in the ocean – the feeling of being at one with nature. But the most exciting part of surfing is the feeling of excitement and anticipation that occurs when you're driving to the beach in the morning, before the sun comes up.

The dawn is quiet and peaceful.

It's still.

Maybe it's the idea of doing something before the rest of the world has even woken up yet that I found solace in. There's something satisfying about the feeling of getting a head start on the rest of the world.

When you first plunge into the ocean water, it's as if you're reborn, and you feel like you've been granted a clean slate. Anything negative that had transpired the day before becomes irrelevant, and the first wave you duck dive under is almost *baptismal*, washing away your transgressions.

In that moment, even if you have a sore back – or in my case, a sore heart – in that moment, your life is *perfect*.

When I wasn't surfing, assuming I wasn't sulking about my divorce, I was trying to get my business off the ground.

I'd often go to a coffee shop up the street from my apartment called *Madre's Coffee House* to get some work done. *Madre's* was usually filled with a bunch of wanna-be's like me.

Wanna-be writers.

Wanna-be entrepreneurs.

Computer geeks.

They all probably thought *I* was as lame as I thought *they* were. I always thought that was kind of funny in an ironic sort of way.

I'd spend several hours at *Madre's* on Saturday mornings.

There was occasionally some pretty good eye candy to look at, not that I had the guts to talk to any of them.

I figured one day, I'd muster up the guts to start dating again, but during that time of my life, I was just focusing on trying to figure out how I was going to turn my small business into a big business.

On one particular Saturday morning, I had a great surf session.

There was practically nobody in the water, and the surf was pretty epic. I caught some exceptionally great waves, and I didn't think about my divorce *once* during the entire time.

Well, maybe I did once or twice.

As I waited for my last wave, I gazed out towards the horizon. For whatever reason, I felt more connected with the ocean that morning.

I was more aware of the water moving in and out between my toes. I was more aware of the salty taste of the ocean's water on my lips. And when I closed my eyes, I could see the warm morning sun's red illumination through my translucent eyelids.

And just then as I opened my eyes, I saw a giant swell forming on the outer break. I paddled swiftly and confidently, putting myself in position, and as the wave began to crest, I effortlessly slid down its face.

The ancient Hawaiians called surfing *he'e nalu* which translated to English means *wave sliding*. Surfing, for the ancient Hawaiians, was somewhat of a sacred practice. It was a time to commune with the *kai* or ocean.

I always felt a special bond with the ocean.

The ocean was powerful and non-discriminating. It could easily kill a man, yet it could also give a man the ride of his life.

The ocean would challenge you, but never judge you. It was never the same – the tides, the currents, the waves – they were never exactly the same.

The ocean would punish you on some days, just to remind you to respect its power. And on other days, it would be completely docile and gentle, allowing you to bathe in its magnificence.

And on special days, it would bless you with the opportunity to ride its mounds of glory – to *he'e nalu*.

This day was such a day.

As I slid down the face of this last wave of the day, I could feel it building in front of me, and as I leaned into the rail of my board, tucking in my knee ever so slightly, I prepared to pull into the *barrel*.

I slid across the wave's glassy face and ran my fingers across it, as it pitched out right over my head.

I was getting barreled or *tubed* as they used to say.

Getting barreled is one of those sacred moments in a surfer's life where the world stops. Literally.

It's a spiritual experience, and ironically, very symbolic of being in a place in life where you feel ultimate happiness.

In the barrel, you're in a place where few men have ever been. That's why they say *Only A Surfer Knows The Feeling*.

The sound of the wave sucking the ocean's water into the liquid tube echoes in a mesmerizing tone. The only sound similar to the sound of being in the tube is the sound that a baby hears in the womb.

You've probably heard that sound when watching a woman receive an ultrasound, anticipating hearing her baby's heartbeat.

It's that consistent, hollow, echoing sound.

Perhaps that's what's so soothing about being inside the barrel. Perhaps it subconsciously reminds us of the safety and self-assuredness we felt being in our mother's womb – back when all of our needs were provided for – back when everyone celebrated our existence.

Back when everyone *marveled* at our mere existence.

It's kind of sad to think that *life* has a way of stripping away those feelings of security.

Maybe that's why I loved surfing so much, getting barreled. It gave me the opportunity to cathartically relive those feelings of unconditional love, security and adoration – things I didn't have in my life as a child – things I surely didn't have in my marriage.

Even though I knew I wasn't the only one on the planet earth in need of unconditional love, in the midst of my depression, it certainly felt like I was. And as a result of my overbearing insecurities, my tendencies were to mask my reality.

A sad reality of the human experience is that we tend to hide from ourselves what we fear we truly are.

And that's what I was doing.

Hiding.

And so I did whatever I could to strive to be more – to be admired and respected. The vast majority of my life's experiences up until that point certainly didn't supply me with very much gratification in regards to such cravings.

And so surfing was my one indulgence – my one great escape from the reality of my afflicted life.

After my surf session, I stopped by my apartment to shower before heading off to *Madre's* – which I called my *satellite office* – to work on designing my new sales brochure.

But something felt different about that morning in particular. I don't know what it was, but something different was in the air.

My vision seemed a little bit clearer.

The air seemed a little bit crisper.

I had an unusual pep in my step.

It was weird, in a good way.

As I placed my order at the coffee shop, there was a gorgeous barista whom I hadn't ever seen before. She was incredibly exotic, of mixed ethnicity. I guessed she was probably part Latin.

She had a beautiful olive complexion and long dark hair, pulled back and tied up in a bun. She wore very little make up, partly because she didn't have to.

Her skin was perfect, and with her high cheekbones and perfect body, she looked like a *Victoria's Secret* supermodel that lost a bet and was forced to wear a *Madre's Coffee* uniform as her punishment.

Strangely, I felt comfortable talking to her as she made my Grande Americano. Normally, I wouldn't have even had the guts to make eye contact with someone that looked like her.

But oddly, as she handed me my coffee, she winked at me and said, "Try our new breakfast sandwich. It's on the house today," as she discreetly handed it to me like we were doing a drug deal in a dark alley.

"What's your name?" I asked.

"I'm Valentina," she said, with an adorable grin. It was cute and sexy all at the same time. She was absolutely mesmerizing.

"Hi, I'm Vincent," I responded.

Even though I wanted to talk with her more, I chickened out, and immediately grabbed a table and sat down.

But I couldn't stop staring at her.

I tried to look cool, sipping my Americano and pretending to look busy.

I wanted to talk to her so badly, but I didn't have the guts to walk back up to the counter and spark up a conversation.

It was busy, and I didn't want to get her in trouble with her boss. At least that's the excuse I convinced myself into believing.

I pretended to be working on my laptop as I watched her out of the corner of my eye. Several hours and several Americanos later, I finally mustered up the courage to go up and talk to her.

I rehearsed in my mind what I would say, over and over.

My palms became balmy as they fidgeted with the paper napkin on the table. I nervously contemplated my approach utilizing my very limited inventory of clever icebreakers. But I figured it was now or never, so I decided to wing it, shooting from the hip.

"Okay, here it goes," I said to myself.

But when I looked up, ready to approach her, she was gone, as if she had magically vanished into thin air. It was a feeling of disappointment and relief all at the same time.

I told myself that I'd come back the following weekend and talk to her then.

All week long, I thought about her.

Okay, I *obsessed* about her.

I rehearsed in my mind exactly what I would say to her when I saw her next.

When Friday night finally came, I went to bed, eagerly anticipating the following morning.

When I woke up Saturday morning, I was like a 12-year old boy on Christmas, ready to rush into the living room and rip open all the presents under the tree.

Excitement and anxiety ferociously pumped through my veins. This was my dream girl.

At 8:05 a.m., I briskly walked into the coffee shop hoping to see Valentina, but she was nowhere to be found.

I stayed there all day, drinking Grande Americano after Grande Americano, hoping that Valentina would walk in the door to start her shift.

By late afternoon, I had downed so many damn Americanos that I was practically pissing Espresso.

Still, no Valentina.

As I continued to work away on my computer, designing my new sales brochure, a strange feeling came over me. It was almost as if the universe was telling me that someone of significance was about to walk in the door.

As I looked up, the door swung open, but it wasn't Valentina.

In walked a tall, distinguished gentleman who looked like a cross between *James Bond* and *Bruce Wayne*.

He wore an exquisitely tailored charcoal grey suit, clearly custom made, and a crisp white Italian dress shirt with a hand-stitched collar.

A uniquely folded white linen pocket square peeked out from behind the large lapel of his suit jacket, so intricately folded that it looked like a Japanese origami master had spent a lifetime designing its presentation.

His hair was slicked back like Andy Garcia's, and he wore dark, mysterious sunglasses... the kind that someone out of a spy movie would wear.

As he walked in, he was so smooth, it looked like he was floating across the room, as if he was moving in slow motion. He had the kind of presence that made him look like he should have had his own soundtrack playing in the background.

I watched him order his drink.

Grande Americano.

Three Splendas.

And a dash of cream.

Ironically, the exact same drink as mine.

The girl that took his order fumbled his receipt, so intimidated by this gentleman, that she knocked over the chocolate bars on display next to the cash register. Same thing with the girl that handed him his Americano, blushing as she sheepishly apologized for being such a klutz.

Amazingly however, the gentleman reassured both of them that it was no big deal, and within a split second, he was able to graciously eliminate any awkwardness that existed.

It was a magical thing to witness.

As I watched this *007ish* episode play out, I thought to myself, "Man, I wish I could be like that."

And just as I said that to myself, the gentleman sat down at the table next to me, looked at me and smiled, and said, "Like what?"

"Huh?" I replied.

"Like what? You wish you could be like what?" the gentleman asked as he looked at me with his all-knowing eyes.

"Oh crap! Did I say that out loud? I thought I said that silently to myself," I embarrassingly blurted out.

I must have had the most mortified expression on my face, because the gentleman started laughing at me, but in a kind-hearted way.

It was the kind of laugh that you make when a 2-year old kid mispronounces the word *frog,* where it sounds like *fock,* which sounds like... well, you know.

"You wish you could be like what?" the gentleman asked again, trying to restrain himself from erupting in laughter.

"Umm, you know, *007 smooth*," I said.

At that moment, he practically spit out his coffee from laughing so hard.

Now I felt like a total idiot.

As I blushed like a little girl, I must have looked completely embarrassed, because he tried to curb his laughter, and apologized for laughing at me.

"I'm sorry. I'm not laughing *at* you. I'm so sorry. I've just never heard the term *007 smooth* before. That's a good one. I'm going to have to steal that one from you," he said as he attempted to catch his breath from laughing so hard.

In an attempt to make me feel better, he further inquired, "What exactly did I do that you thought was so smooth?"

"The way those girls practically melted when you looked at them. They looked at you like you were some kind of movie star or something. Girls never look at me like that," I explained.

I continued, "And then once they made fools of themselves, you made them feel okay... comfortable and safe. You took an awkward situation and made everything cool in like five seconds. It was like magic."

At that point, I was unaware that I had abandoned any verbal filter I may have had. I kept going.

"When you walked in the door, it was like you commanded everyone's respect before you even opened your mouth. Man, you're like *James Bond*! Oh my God. I can't believe I just said that. I'm such an idiot," I embarrassingly apologized.

At that point, the gentleman had transitioned from uncontrollable laughter to empathetic intrigue.

He said, "Look kid, I don't think you're an idiot. It's okay."

As I regained my composure, he put his hand on my shoulder and said, "I think I know what you're trying to say. Let me explain what you saw me do. Yes, I do have that effect on a lot of people. They get intimidated by my *007 smoothness* as you put it."

He then said, "Just out of curiosity, what kind of work do you do?"

I told him I used to be a high school teacher, but I really wanted to be an entrepreneur.

I explained, "Two years ago, I started a small business selling nutritional supplements… you know, vitamins and stuff."

I didn't tell him any details about my dismal business.

At that time, I wasn't even making enough money to pay my bills. In fact, I was living off credit card cash advances, doing balance transfers every time a credit card company came out with a new promotional interest rate.

I was eating oatmeal and *Top Ramen* noodles for dinner every night, because that's all I could afford at that time.

I was broke.

I told him that I had recently been divorced, and that I was just now getting back on my feet, starting my life over.

For whatever reason, he seemed genuinely interested and compassionate towards me about my story.

He asked me very detailed questions about my life.

He asked me questions about my business venture and why I thought it wasn't as successful as I'd hoped.

I didn't even tell him that my business was struggling, but by the lack of confidence I exuded, I guess he could tell.

We talked for a good twenty minutes.

He finally said, "I've got to run. It was great meeting you, but before I go, I've got a proposition for you."

"H-huh?" I stuttered.

"What's your name, kid?" he asked.

"Uh, Vincent," I replied.

"Vincent, you're a mess… and I'm going to help you," he offered.

I had read a self-help book recently that talked about the value of having a mentor – someone that you could emulate – that was willing to teach you how to be successful.

I thought to myself, "Maybe this is my chance."

Then he said seven words that changed my life forever…

1. Meet
2. Me
3. Here
4. Tomorrow
5. Morning
6. At
7. 8:00 a.m.

Chapter Two
The First Day Of The Rest Of My Life

As I stared at my alarm clock, it was 4:17 a.m., Sunday morning. I had set my alarm clock for 7:30 a.m., giving me just enough time to shower and head down to the coffee shop to meet the mysterious gentleman I had met the day before.

I was actually used to waking up before my alarm clock went off, and as usual, I couldn't go back to sleep.

But on this morning, it was for a different reason.

I was actually excited.

It felt like the kind of excitement I had when I woke up early in the morning to go surfing.

Tons of questions zip lined through my brain.

What was this guy going to teach me?

Why did he want to help me?

Would he help me get Valentina's phone number?

Would he make me a job offer?

I remember thinking to myself, "I hope I don't blow this."

As I got dressed, I started heading down the road to *Negative Land*, hanging a right onto *Pessimist Boulevard*, worrying about what might or might not happen.

What if he didn't show up?

What if he disappeared like Valentina did?

What if he thought I was a loser, like my ex-wife did?

This guy was definitely a multi-millionaire. You could just tell by the way he carried himself. I didn't ask him what kind of work he did, but I was sure he was making a ton of money. He just exuded power – the kind of power that comes with wealth.

I thought to myself, "Why would a guy at this level want to meet with me? I'm a nobody."

I was doing it again, being *Mr. Negative.*

"Stop it!" I told myself.

The motivational audio program I was listening to in my car kept telling me to stop self-sabotaging everything in my life. It told me to stop expecting the worst, and to always expect the best.

Easier said than done.

Sometimes, when I was in one of my self-loathing moods, I'd actually flick off the CD player in my car with my middle finger as the self-help audio program told me to take charge of my life.

But for some reason, I kept forcing myself to listen to it.

In all honesty, sometimes that audio program was the only thing that kept me going. Practically everyone else in my life was telling me to quit, give up on my dream, and just go get a regular cubicle job.

But the self-help guru in the motivational CD program kept telling me to go for it.

I don't know very many people that have had interactive conversations with motivational audio CD programs, but I had them regularly in my car. People driving by me on the freeway probably thought I had Tourette's syndrome or something.

In any case, it was time to head off to my meeting.

As I walked up to the coffee shop, he was already there, sipping his Grande Americano, with three Splendas and a dash of cream. He was leaning up against the hottest Lamborghini I'd ever seen. This thing looked like *The Bat Mobile.*

"He IS Bruce Wayne! I knew it!" I said to myself.

"Nice ride," I said in my overly impressed voice.

Without taking off his sunglasses, he looked at his rose gold *IWC DaVinci* watch, and said, "You're late. *Rule Number One: Don't ever be late...* especially to a meeting with me."

"Umm, I'm sorry. I thought you said to meet you here at 8:00 a.m. It's only 7:56 a.m.," I apologetically and embarrassingly responded.

"Rule Number One, Part A: Don't ever be late. Rule Number One, Part B: If you're not at least 15 minutes early… then you're late," he said as he removed his sunglasses in slow motion, his eyes piercing into mine.

The power that he exuded was frightening. I wish he had kept his shades on, because the look he had in his eyes scared the living daylights out of me.

It was like the ocean. You respect it, and even though you fear it, you also want to be close to it. As I attempted to apologize for not knowing the rules, he cut me off.

"I'm not upset, kid. I'm just letting you know the rules. If you want to roll with me, you've got to play by my rules. Let's grab a seat over here," he said as he handed me a freshly brewed Grande Americano with three Splendas and a dash of cream.

In an attempt to sound like I was part of the club, I said, "Cool that we drink the same kind of coffee, huh?"

Without even looking at me, he said, "They're not the same. Mine has an extra shot of Espresso in it."

"Really! Maybe I should try that sometime," I gushed.

"No, you're not ready for all that, kid. I'll let you know when you're ready," he said, putting me in my place.

Everything he did – everything he said – was thought out to the Nth degree, and as we began to talk, I realized that this guy was the most diabolical, system-driven person I had ever met. He wasn't just incredibly smart – brilliant actually – but he was also aware of his every move, and aware of everyone else's every move around him.

"So you never actually told me how you were able to diffuse the awkwardness of the situation with those two cute chicks that work here, you know, the ones that were all ga-ga over you yesterday," I reminded him.

"I know," he curtly replied.

Expecting him to unveil his magic secrets to me, he just stared at me with a relaxed, yet confident grin. Several seconds elapsed that felt like several minutes.

"Okay, before I tell you how I diffused that uncomfortable situation, let me ask you why you think I had that affect on them in the first place," he inquired.

"Umm, I dunno," I mumbled.

"Rule Number Two: Don't ever let your brain be lazy. When someone asks you a question, think about it thoroughly. A lazy man quickly responds by saying *'I dunno'* not because he can't figure it out, but rather because he doesn't want to take the time to TRY to figure it out," he explained.

"Seriously," he said. "Think through this. I get that kind of reaction from people everywhere I go. I even got it from you. And I get these reactions before I even open my mouth to speak. So what did I do to impress you within the first five seconds?"

"Umm, the way you dress," I replied.

"What about the way I dress?" he asked.

"You know, you're wearing a suit that looks like it's custom made and costs about $3,000," I said.

"This one costs over $8,000," he said, quickly correcting me.

He pointed at me and said, "Look at you. You aren't even dressed for business. You knew you were coming here to meet me, and you're dressed like every other average guy in here."

"Umm, this is a *Greg Norman* golf shirt. This is the nicest golf shirt I have. It costs over $100," I said in an attempt to defend my wardrobe.

"Do you know why they call them *Golf Shirts*? They call them *Golf Shirts* because you're supposed to wear them when you go golfing," he proclaimed in a semi-cynical tone of voice.

He continued, "All this talk about *Business Casual* is just plain stupid. It's for lazy people that don't want to take the time to dress properly for business. I know that *everyone* dresses more casually now days, but the question is, do you want to be like everyone else – underdressed and broke – or do you want to have the effect on people that I have?" he asked.

Obviously, he knew that I knew the answer to that question.

"Vincent, it's time you learned *Rule Number Three: If you want what average people have, do what they do.* If you want to have what I have, do what I do."

He continued, "You see, most people are *sheeple.* They're like sheep that have the *herd mentality*, which is why they live mediocre lives. If you do the same things they do, you're sure to end up with the same things they have, and I'm assuming your goal is not to be mediocre."

I had never really thought about it like that before. I was so caught up in other people's opinions of me, especially my father's. And the irony was that none of these people that criticized me were living the life that I dreamed about having for myself.

That's what this gentleman was trying to get me to see.

It was like he was performing Lasik surgery on my eyes – eyes that so severely lacked *clarity of sight*. He would eventually work on my brain too – a brain that so severely lacked *clarity of thought*.

He told me, "You see Vincent, in order to achieve greatness, you've got to take a *different* path than everyone else. And as you're experiencing, the social pressure to conform to the masses is stronger than you think."

He certainly didn't succumb to any sort of social norms or social pressures, yet he acknowledged the fact that he was an emotional human being. The difference was that his principles overrode his emotions.

He was definitely a man of principle.

He explained, "Human beings, at our core, want to be accepted, ironically, by the masses. When you think through this, it makes no sense. What do we care what the masses think about us? They don't live the kind of lives that we want to live. They don't aspire to achieve greatness. But for some strange and illogical reason, we secretly seek their approval. That's why you have to make a conscious effort not to succumb to their silly social pressures."

He was right.

I cared far too much about what other people thought of me, and I was incredibly insecure.

That was the bad news.

The good news was that I was honest enough to admit it.

I wanted to live above the imprisoned mindset of caring about what other people thought about me. He clearly wasn't a prisoner obsessed with other people's opinions of him. Perhaps it was easier for him to do because he was already incredibly successful.

However the more I listened to his lessons, the more I realized that he learned these lessons through making his own mistakes.

He was, indeed, human.

He would share with me how he started off his career as a struggling entrepreneur, and he understood the emotions I was going through – the emotional struggles of self-doubt and overwhelming stress. That's one of the many things that made him such a great mentor.

He *understood* me.

He explained, "Whenever you venture outside the norm, you're going to be judged harshly, and you're going to be faced with heavy criticism from other people. But in order to become great, you've got to have the guts to buck the system. You've got to be willing to do what most people are not willing to do… and when you do this, you'll have what most people will never have."

As much uncertainty as I had in my life during that time, there was one thing I *was* certain of. I didn't want to live a life of mediocrity.

I wanted more.

"Vincent, you'll never soar with the eagles if you spend your time conforming to what the pigeons do. In nature, you'll never see a flock of eagles soaring high in the sky. Eagles soar alone. The only time where you see more than one eagle flying together is during the mating process... and they only mate with other eagles," said my newfound mentor.

I immediately thought about my ex-wife.

She was definitely not an eagle.

"And it's not just your mindset. When it comes to the way you dress, it's no different. You've got these schmucks out there that brag about how they don't wear suits and ties anymore. It makes me laugh. They've got their *Tommy Bahama* shirts on, looking like they're going to a Hawaiian luau. In reality, they look like THEY should be the one roasting in the ground instead of the pig," he said as he rolled his eyes with a half smile.

At this point, I couldn't tell if he was actually upset or if he was just poking fun at his contemporaries.

"Look, there's nothing necessarily wrong with dressing like everyone else, but if you want to walk into a room and command the level of respect and intrigue that you witnessed me commanding yesterday, the best way to do it is to wear a beautifully tailored suit," he continued.

"I have all my suits custom made by my tailor in Milan, Italy. I've got it dialed in with this guy. In fact, the one I was wearing yesterday was also made by him."

"Wow, that's awesome," I replied. "How would I get a hold of him?"

"You wouldn't. He works for me. I own the company," he explained.

"Ohhhh, so you're in the fashion business?" I inquired.

"That's one of my companies," he replied.

"How many companies do you own?" I asked.

"Six," he replied.

I stuttered, "S… S… Six companies? How do you manage all of that? I can barely manage one… and I'm not even doing THAT very well."

"We'll get to that much later," he replied. "So the first way to capture someone's attention is to dress in a manner that exudes confidence and success, and nothing tells that story better than a well tailored suit. I started that company because I wanted to create the kind of clothing that I like to wear. Unique pieces. Bespoke pieces. Our clients are the type of people that want to wear suits that no one else has… suits that no one else can get, regardless of how much money they have. That's what grabs people's attention at first glance. It certainly grabbed your attention yesterday."

He was right. I began to get the feeling that he was always right. Maybe not *always*, but certainly most of the time.

"Now, a beautifully tailored suit certainly commands attention, but you've also got to have *substance* and *talent* to back it up. If you take an idiot and put him in an $8,000 custom suit, all you've got is a well dressed idiot," he explained.

He never came across as a *Mr. Know-It-All*, but when it came to business and dealing with people, he was brilliant to say the least.

He said, "Think about this. It's kind of like when you walk into a room at a party, or a bar or club. Girls are going to notice the guy that stands out, and the most noticeable way to stand out initially is the way you dress."

He went on to say, "If everyone else dresses the same, and you're dressed just like them, girls are going to assume you're just another average guy. Do you really think girls get excited about meeting *Mr. Average*? Of course not."

I jumped in and said, "Yeah, I saw this guy on TV that claimed he could double the number of chicks I get. He even had a DVD program about how to do it… and he said one of the ways to do it is to wear something outrageous… a conversation piece."

"Like what?" he asked.

"You know, like a pink feather boa... or a weird hat."

He then looked at me with a condescending smile. It was the way you look at an 8-year old kid wearing a Batman Halloween costume... in February.

"Let me ask you a question," he said. "Are you looking to just get laid, or are you looking to attract a particular type of woman?"

I felt like a total idiot, not knowing how to respond.

Truthfully, I never really thought about the question he was asking me. However as I began to think about it on a deeper level, I realized that it was incredibly stupid of me to have never identified what I really wanted.

As I told him that deciphering the difference between the two had never crossed my mind, he broke out into a gregarious laugh, almost falling out of his chair.

"Look," he said. "If you don't know what kind of fish you're trying to catch, then how are you going to know what kind of bait to use? If you want a party chick, go ahead and wear the feather boa and the Dr. Seuss hat. But if you want a sophisticated woman, you should be dressing more sophisticated. You've got to consciously dress to attract the woman of your dreams."

He went on to say, "Before I met my wife, my social attire consisted of distressed jeans, flip-flops and t-shirts. I wore suits and ties everyday for business, but on the weekends, I dressed like a guy ready to party at the bar by the beach. There was nothing wrong with dressing like that, but I was attracting all the hot, young chicks that wanted to party. Again, nothing wrong with that... in fact, it was pretty fun for a while."

"Young, hot chicks that want to party? Sounds good to me!" I exclaimed.

"On the surface, I would agree with you. But the problem was that I didn't want to be a player anymore. I'd already done that, and it left me very unfulfilled. Again, I'm not saying that there's anything wrong with living that lifestyle. The point is – the most important point – is that it wasn't the lifestyle that *I* personally wanted anymore. I wanted to settle down and start a family," he explained.

"So what did you do?" I asked.

"Well, the first thing I did was write out a detailed list of all the qualities that I wanted in a wife. The list was over one and a half pages long. And when I got done, I asked myself if I was embodying the persona that a woman like that would be attracted to. Now, in some areas, I was. But in others, I was not. And that revelation sparked the change in the way I started dressing on the weekends," he said.

"So what was on your list?" I asked.

"Are you asking me that question because you're curious as to what I think is important in a woman, or because you want my advice on what you should be looking for?" he asked me.

"Uhhh, isn't that the same thing?" I said.

Just as those words left my mouth, I realized that every question he asked was intended to better clarify an important distinction. Behind every one of his questions was a life lesson to be learned... a life lesson that was intended to bring about a life-changing epiphany.

He said, "Seeking *alternative perspectives* and seeking *advice* are two entirely different things. I'm happy to share with you my perspective on what's important to me, but what's important to ME may be different than what's important to YOU. What I think you should be looking for in a woman is irrelevant. The only thing that's relevant is what's right for YOU."

And so he grilled me again, asking, "So which one is it?"

"Ummm, I guess I'm curious about your perspective," I mumbled.

"Why?" he asked, crossing his arms.

"Because you seem like you're happy. You seem like you've got all the answers... like you've got everything figured out," I said.

He broke out into another one of his over-the-top, gregarious laughs.

He said, "Well, I don't have it ALL figured out, but I HAVE figured out some things... and one of them is *Rule Number Four: Seek different perspectives, but never ask for advice.*"

"You see, when you ask for advice, you're essentially saying three things. One, you're assuming that the other person knows your situation better than you, which is just plain stupid. Two, you're assuming the other person is better at figuring out what's most important to you, which is equally as stupid. And three, you're being irresponsible, pushing the responsibility of making the right decision onto someone else... which creates the opportunity to blame them if things don't pan out right. If you add up these two assumptions and one cop-out, all you get is the depiction of a weak man," he explained.

His amused countenance gradually transitioned into an incredibly intense and serious mood, as he stared at me the way a boxer stares down his opponent before a fight.

He intimidated the heck out of me.

But everything he said, I knew was right.

Then it dawned on me.

I would never get another chance to learn from someone so wise. This was my golden opportunity to turn my life around.

In life, if you're extremely lucky, you get blessed with a life changing opportunity, and that opportunity usually comes in the form of a mentor.

Most people never get the opportunity to truly be mentored by someone that has achieved greatness, and this – this chance meeting with this incredibly powerful and successful gentleman – was my once-in-a-lifetime opportunity.

One thing puzzled me though.

Why was he willing to spend this time with me?

I'm pretty sure he had more important things to do than meet me at a coffee shop on a Sunday morning.

And so I asked him point blank, "Why are you doing this?"

"Doing what?" he asked.

"This. Meeting with me. Teaching me this stuff. Why are you trying to help me?" I asked as my voice quivered.

I got a heavy feeling in my heart, and my eyes started to well up with tears. I hung my head in shame and embarrassment.

As my voice trembled, I told him, "No one's ever taken an interest in me. No one's ever extended themselves to me like this, offering to help me. Not even my dad."

It was as if he felt my pain.

He said, "Kid, you kind of remind me of someone. I'll just leave it at that for now."

He never did tell me what was on his list of qualities he wanted in a wife. Perhaps I had overstepped my boundaries. Or maybe he wanted me to come up with my own list.

I figured he had his reasons.

As we talked, I slowly began to notice that he talked very little, and that I was the one doing most of the talking.

He asked me questions about how I grew up, what kind of relationships I'd had over the years, why I thought my marriage fell apart, and why I felt my business wasn't progressing at the rate I wanted it to.

About an hour had passed, but it seemed like the time had just flown by. As he finished the last sip of his Americano, he put his hand on my shoulder as he stood up, and said, "Alright. I'm prepared to take you on, kid."

"Take me on?" I said in a confused tone.

"Kid, you're lost right now. You don't have any clarity as to what you want to create in your life... who you want to be... or who you want to be with. And I'm guessing this business of yours isn't where you want it to be either," he said.

That pretty much summed up my life at that point. He was dead on. I wanted to figure it all out, like he seemed to have it all figured out.

I felt like I was just meandering through life. I was walking fast, but I wasn't going anywhere, and I needed direction.

I think that was the only thing in my life I was certain of. I thought to myself, "This is my chance to finally have a mentor."

He then told me, "Vincent, we're going to get your act together, and if you're lucky, I may even be able to help you with your career too."

I walked him back to his *Bat Mobile* inspired Lamborghini, and as he climbed inside the cockpit, without even looking at me, he said, "I have someone I want you to meet. Meet me back here next Saturday at 8:00 a.m.… and don't be late."

As he drove away, I wondered who this mystery person was that he wanted me to meet.

Was he going to fix me up on a blind date?

What if Valentina happened to be working that day? Would that be awkward?

And then I chuckled to myself.

I realized I'd probably never see Valentina ever again, and even if I did, I don't even know if I'd have the guts to talk to her.

I had to adjust to this new world – the world of being single again – and even though I had obviously been single before, the game had changed.

Man, did I feel like a fish out of water, but I believed that this mysterious new mentor of mine could teach me how to convert my gills into lungs.

Chapter Three
Andrei The Protégé

The next week was perhaps the slowest week of my entire life. I had a few sales appointments, but most of them were exercises in futility.

I could barely even concentrate on what I was doing, due to anxiously awaiting my next encounter with my new mentor.

I must admit, I did stop by the coffee shop once or twice during the week to see if Valentina was working.

Okay, the truth is, I stopped by every morning.

I know that makes me sound like a desperate stalker, but I couldn't help it. Confidence, at that particular point in my life, was not at an all time high. I wasn't going to win *The Cockiest Man Of The Year Award*, that's for sure.

Finally, the week came to an end – five days of covertly stalking Valentina – and five days of inconsequential sales appointments. Despite my lack of results from both efforts, I found myself with an abundance of energy and positivity as the weekend approached.

Before I went to bed Friday night, I remembered what the *James Bond-esque* gentleman said about dressing appropriately for a given occasion. I didn't know who he would be introducing me to on Saturday morning at the coffee shop, but I figured it would require me to make an impression.

I pulled out my best white, button-down collar dress shirt, my one and only blazer, and a pair of black slacks.

I tried on my outfit that evening to see what I looked like. My jacket was a little too big, which looked sloppy compared to a tailored jacket. My slacks were a little too baggy too.

I definitely didn't look like anything that resembled *James Bond* or *Bruce Wayne*, but at the time, that was all I could afford.

I set my alarm clock an hour and a half before my meeting. I would not violate *Rule Number One, Part A* or *Part B*, ever again.

With my wardrobe ready to go, neatly hanging on the doorknob of my bathroom door, I confidently went to sleep that night, anticipating that something special might happen the next morning.

I woke up that next morning, put on my outfit like I was putting on my battle armor, and walked down to the coffee shop.

I arrived at 7:43 a.m., two minutes before the required 15-minute early expectation. I didn't see him in the coffee shop or in the parking lot. No Bat Mobile.

"Ah ha! I beat him here!" I gloated to myself.

But just as I began to do my happy dance, a young, Eastern European gentleman stepped out of a matte black Porsche Turbo GT.

He looked me up and down, and said, "Let me guess. You're Vincent."

"Uhh, yeah, I am," I said.

"So you're the kid *The Icon* wanted me to meet," he said.

"The Icon?" I asked, completely puzzled.

"Yeah, bro. That's what we all call him. That's *who* he is. That's *what* he is. Anyway, first off, you're late," the Eastern European gentleman said as he walked towards me.

I quickly figured out that this was the individual The Icon wanted me to meet.

"I thought you already learned *Rule Number One*," he accusatorily said.

I defensively, yet humbly said, "I'm sorry. I thought *Rule Number One* was to be fifteen minutes early."

"*Rule Number One* is to always be TWENTY minutes early," he said as he walked towards the entrance of the coffee shop. As he entered through the doors, he had the same float-across-the-room kind of walk as The Icon did.

He smiled at the cute girl at the cash register (who was NOT Valentina by the way), and held up two fingers, saying not a word, as he walked to a table in the back of the coffee shop.

As we sat down, the young, flashy gentleman said, "I'm Andrei. I understand you're a total mess."

"Well, I don't know if I'm a TOTAL mess," I clarified.

"Bro, that wasn't a question. It's an obvious fact," Andrei said in his Romanian accent.

Andrei was a young guy, just a few years older than me. Thirty-one or thirty-two years old, I would guess. He was dressed almost exactly the same as The Icon.

Blue pinstriped suit.

White pocket square.

Italian loafers. Very *expensive* Italian loafers.

His hair was slicked back, just like The Icon*'s*.

It was like I was looking at a *Mini-Icon*, but I didn't dare call him that. There was nothing *mini* about Andrei. By the size of this guy, he looked like he could pretty much bench press my car.

Five minutes later, two Americanos showed up at our table, as the cute girl announced, "Gentlemen, two Grande Americanos... three Spendas each, with a dash of cream... and an extra shot of Espresso for yours, Andrei."

I submitted to the fact that I was going to have to earn the right to get that extra shot of Espresso.

"Listen, I'm hosting a charity brunch event at 10:00 a.m., so let's cut to the chase. I understand you're a total mess, and that The Icon chose you as his new Protégé. Congratulations," Andrei said.

"H-huh?" I stammered.

"Bro, Don't ever say *huh?* It makes you sound f***in' stupid and unsure of yourself," said Andrei.

Without dwelling on my foot-in-mouth reaction, Andrei said, "Bro, you're the new Protégé."

I must have had a dumbfounded look on my face.

Andrei said, "You don't know how it works, do you."

I already knew that Andrei wasn't asking me a question.

This was definitely a stated fact.

Andrei explained, "About every eight to ten years, The Icon takes on a new protégé – someone to personally mentor – assuming he thinks he can turn their life around. He chose you. You're the new Protégé. Eight years ago, he chose me."

He went on to say, "Bro, ten years ago, I was fresh off the plane from Romania. My English sucked ass, man. My father spent his entire life savings to send me to America – to *make it* in America. The problem was, I didn't have no f***in' clue what I was doing. I met The Icon when I was only twenty-four years old, two years after I landed here in America. I met him in a coffee shop, kinda like you did. Totally random, man. But the difference was that I was *working* at the coffee shop. I was just gettin' off my shift, and when I cleared the last table, I saw the customer was gonna throw away a sandwich they barely even touched. I snatched that sh** on the down low, and put it in my pocket, and I guess The Icon saw me do it," Andrei confessed.

"Bro, I barely made enough money at my sh***y job at the coffee shop to pay my bills, and so I usually tried to get my hands on food that customers were gonna throw away, and that's what I'd eat for dinner. The Icon stopped me in the parking lot when I was walkin' to my car. I thought this guy was gonna f***in' bust me or something," Andrei said, as he cracked an ever-so-subtle smile. This was the first time I saw him even grin, excluding greeting the cute girl behind the cash register.

As Andrei explained to me his first encounter with The Icon, he communicated with such enthusiasm – with such vigor. He was raw in his tone, and equally as raw in communicating every little detail, dropping an F-bomb about every 2.7 seconds. Andrei just told it like it was, with no filter whatsoever.

Andrei explained, "When The Icon came up to me and told me he saw me grab that sandwich off that customer's plate, I said *'What, you got a f***in' problem with that, bro?'* and I got up in his face. He didn't even flinch. He just smiled at me and said, *'First of all, I'm not your bro, get it? And second of all, I'm not trying to judge you, son. I'm curious because I want to help you.'*"

The Icon wasn't the kind of man to sink to a low level bar fight or street brawl. He was above such nonsense, but he carried himself in a way that let you know that it was in your best interest to treat him with ultimate respect.

The Icon was intimidated by no one, not even Andrei.

And trust me, Andrei was intimidating.

Andrei shared with me how The Icon took him under his wing, helping him get his business off the ground.

"Bro, I thought The Icon was f***in' crazy. Why would this rich-ass motherf***er want to help me?" Andrei exclaimed.

Andrei grew up in a family that would wait in line for three days, just to get meat – something not easily accessible in his home town in Romania.

His friends back home were thugs, and so his father sent him to America to build a better life – a better future.

"I didn't have no f***in' track record of success, bro. I was makin' minimum wage working at a coffee shop, you know what I mean? But I impressed The Icon 'cause I was driven. Bro, I used to pick up his f***in' dry cleaning for him, you know what I'm sayin'? I used to wash his car for him. I did whatever I had to do to stay on his radar, 'cause I knew he was my ticket to success. All I was lookin' for was an opportunity and a mentor... and all The Icon was lookin' for was a kid with some motherf***in' guts," Andrei explained.

He continued, "I started off as The Icon's personal assistant. But he didn't treat me like no personal assistant, bro. He treated me like a mentee – like a Protégé. He taught me how to deal with people. Then he taught me how to *sell*. Then he taught me how to put together a business deal. And eventually, he taught me how to run the show."

"But first, I had to prove myself to him. I worked seven days a week, sixteen hours a day. I never took no days off work, even when The Icon told me to. I told him I wasn't gonna take no days off until I proved to him that he could trust me – I'm talkin' trust me with *everything*. It took me four years to prove myself to him. That's when he offered me a partnership," Andrei went on.

"Bro, I was only twenty-eight years old back then. Today, I'm thirty-two, and I'm a partner in his luxury custom jewelry company. I'm a f***in' millionaire because of him. I owe him my life," Andrei told me.

He continued, "It's like this, bro. If you wanna be successful, you gotta figure out three things. The *What*, the *Why*, and the *How*. First off, tell me your *What*. What's the most important thing you want in your life?"

I paused for a moment, and said, "I want to be successful and make lots of money, but that isn't what's really the most important to me. What I really want in my life was *respect*. I mean, sure I want respect from other people, but I want self-respect."

I hung my head low as I confessed to Andrei my feelings of worthlessness. I wanted to feel good about myself, and up until that point in my life, I had never felt good about myself.

Andrei jumped in and said, "Bro, don't even worry about that. The Icon's gonna help you out with that one. He got me to believe in myself, and I came from nuthin' man."

He continued, "Okay, so that's your *what*. Now tell me your *why*. Why's that so important to you?" Andrei questioned.

"I guess it's because I've never had that feeling of confidence. I've never really felt good about myself. Partly because my father always put me down. Partly because my ex-wife put me down. I just want to feel good about myself," I shamefully admitted.

Andrei listened to me. I mean, he *really* listened to me.

As I explained to him how tormented my soul had become as a result of my tormented past, Andrei intensely stared into my eyes. Intrigued and captivated by my story, he tapped his index finger on the tip of his goatee-covered chin as he plotted my revenge.

He took a moment to respond after I had spent the last fifteen minutes telling him about my insecurities. He looked as though he was mentally organizing the details of my story to fully understand what I had been through.

He then said, "Okay, Vincent. Check it out, bro. I never used to feel good about myself either. It ain't nuthin' to be ashamed of, alright. You think I jumped off the plane from Romania with all this swagger you see right here? No way, bro. I used to feel like a f***in' loser, you know what I'm sayin'? I wasn't quite as f***ed up as you are, but I was still pretty f***ed. I wanted revenge on all them people out there that said I wasn't ever gonna be nuthin'. Sounds like you want revenge on your ex-wife too. That's good. That's a good motivator."

It was hard to imagine Andrei without his cocky swagger.

"Okay, Vincent. You got your *What* and your *Why*. Now you gotta put your *How* together. In other words, you gotta figure out how you're gonna make all this happen. That's where you're f***ed right now. You ain't got no game plan, bro. That's what The Icon did for me. He helped me put together my *How*. If you ain't got your *How* down, I don't care how motivated you are, you ain't ever gonna be sh**!" Andrei exclaimed

He continued, "Cause if you're motivated, and you're a f***in' idiot, then all you are is a motivated idiot with no plan. You gotta have a plan of *how* you're gonna make all this sh** happen, you understand?"

I clearly didn't have my *How* down.

Sure I wanted to be successful, and I had a ton of solid motivating factors that made me vigilant in my pursuit of success, but I had no idea how to make it all happen. In fact, I didn't even know what the first step was.

"Look here bro. I can tell you wanna blow up and become successful. Just remember one thing. All those people out there that made you feel like you ain't ever gonna be sh** – including your ex-wife – all of them are gonna be eatin' their f***in' words when you make it, bro. If you're rolling with The Icon, all you gotta do is give him 100% of your best effort, and he'll show you how to become successful. He'll develop your *How*," Andrei confidently explained.

My time with Andrei flew by incredibly fast, and by the time we finished our conversation, I felt a kinship with him.

I thought to myself, if The Icon got Andrei to where he is today, maybe he could do the same for me.

Part of me thought it sounded too good to be true, but another part of me hoped that I might be able to follow in Andrei's footsteps.

I've always been a dreamer, believing that one day, I'd be incredibly successful. The problem was at that point in my life, I had nothing to show for it.

There was no hint of progress in my life.

But the glimmer of hope that The Icon gave me was enough to keep me going, even if Valentina didn't show up behind the counter that day either.

"Oh yeah, one last thing. *Rule Number Five: The greatest pleasure in life is accomplishing things that other people said you couldn't do.* Remember that one. Especially when it comes to your ex-wife that dogged you out, bro. ESPECIALLY her. As long as you don't f*** things up with The Icon, and as long as you don't give him no bullsh** excuses, he's gonna make you a superstar. He did it for me, and I ain't the only protégé he's done it with. And your ex-wife... Vincent, let me tell you something bro... that b**** is gonna eat her words, bro. One day, she's gonna realize that leavin' you was the biggest f***in' mistake of her life," Andrei said as if he were prophesizing.

As abrasive and politically incorrect as Andrei was, I kind of liked him. He was candid and raw. He didn't pull any punches. He was one of those guys that you either loved or hated, and even if you hated him, you had to love his brutal honesty.

There was no false pretense about Andrei whatsoever. No sugar coating. No nonsense.

I wasn't necessarily a fan of his abrasiveness, but I would grow to respect his transparency.

Right before Andrei departed, he told me, "The Icon wants you to meet him at a hotel in Beverly Hills called '*The Hotel 100*' tomorrow at 3:00 p.m. sharp. It's on Wilshire Boulevard, right off Rodeo Drive. And don't be f***in' late, bro."

I knew this meant 2:40 p.m., according to Andrei's version of *Rule Number One, Part B*.

Chapter Four
Luxury With A Capital L

I wasn't taking any chances. I showed up at 2:30 p.m., thirty minutes before the actual meeting time.

I parked four blocks away on the street because the valet parking was $18 at the hotel. That was pretty standard pricing for parking in Beverly Hills, and definitely outside of my budget.

The entrance to the hotel was magnificent. The ceilings were all hand painted, like something you'd see in *The Basilica*. The floors consisted of the most intricate Italian marble inlay I'd ever seen and the walls were immaculately finished in Venetian plaster throughout the entire grand lobby.

As I approached the concierge, it became obvious to me that this was how I wanted to live... the life of luxury.

This was *Luxury*, with a capital *L*.

The concierge smiled and said, "You must be Vincent. Welcome to *The Hotel 100*. We've been expecting you. My name is Francisco."

It seemed as though The Icon had the entire world on his payroll. It appeared that the universe revolved around his agenda, and everyone seemed happy to be orbiting around him.

Francisco motioned to one of his assistants and said, "Please escort Mr. Vincent to the Presidential Suite."

I followed Francisco's assistant into the elevator, and as we ascended to the top floor, I wondered what a *Presidential Suite* in a hotel of this stature would look like.

As I entered the suite, I felt like I was in a movie.

The suite had its own foyer.

Baby grand piano.

Three fireplaces.

Formal dining room.

This place was no joke.

I entered the living room and sat down on a crushed velvet sofa – a sofa that looked too expensive to sit on. Its color was a deep magenta, but when a piece of furniture is this luxurious, you don't call the color *deep magenta*. You call it something more exotic, like *merlot* or *chianti*. It looked like something that was auctioned by *Sotheby's* for more than that cost of a condo in Brentwood.

I visually scoured the room, admiring each individual piece of furniture, art and accouterment that so marvelously enhanced the other. The attention to detail was spectacular, clearly the work of a master designer.

The Icon walked into the living room area to greet me.

"Vincent! Running a bit early, I see. I like that," he said, extending his hand to shake mine.

I quickly stood up and replied, "Well, Andrei told me that I should be 20 minutes early in order to be on time, so I figured I'd make it 30 minutes, just to be safe."

"Good thinking. You know, you can never be too early. *Rule Number One* is so simple, but incredibly important. Great men are respecters of time, because time is one thing that you can never get back. If you lose money, you can always make it back. If you lose a material possession, you can always replace it. But once you've lost time, that moment is gone forever. And if you're late, you might miss out on a great opportunity, because sometimes life, as well as people, won't wait for you," The Icon explained.

I understood what he was so artfully communicating to me. Without overtly spelling it out for me, The Icon was telling me this opportunity that I was being afforded was special. He obviously could have just bluntly told me, but that wasn't The Icon's style. He always got his point across by telling insightful stories – stories that made me think about life from a more global perspective.

The Icon motioned to me to have a seat back on the merlot velvet sofa, as he sat down in an equally as impressive caribou suede chair.

He continued, "In addition, being late will ultimately become part of your personal brand. It sends a message to those around you that you can't be counted on. It may seem unimportant, and perhaps the majority of the time, being a little late is inconsequential, but it plants a seed in people's minds that you don't take things very seriously. In all areas of your life, but especially in business, you can't afford to be perceived as such. When you're late, people will perceive that you don't place a very high level of importance on the event in question, and if that event can start without your immediate presence, and it does, the person who makes the decision to *start* without you will most likely be willing to *continue* without you. They'll definitely continue the event without you, and possibly continue in business without you, leaving you behind. Vincent, a word to the wise: If the meeting can *start* without you, the business can *continue* without you. Don't get left behind in the dust due to the irresponsibility of showing up late."

His message was loud and clear, but he continued to elaborate, which told me that tardiness was one of his biggest pet peeves.

"Vincent, you should always give yourself at least twenty minutes of buffer time. There are two main reasons for this. One, it gives you some time to mentally prepare – to do some *mental calisthenics* – prior to performing. Athletes always spend time warming up, just prior to performing. A baseball player takes several practice swings before he steps up to the plate, visualizing his success, and practicing his timing. A great athlete prepares to perform, and in business, you also need to prepare to perform. No world-class athlete jumps off the bench without warming up and attempts to perform with no preparation. Neither should you when it comes to a business meeting."

This made complete sense to me. Even though I wasn't a very talented baseball player as a kid, I would watch Major League ball games on TV and study the intensity of the players,

51

especially in the on-deck circle. They would both physically and mentally prepare to perform.

"Vincent, you may look at some of your business meetings and rationalize that some meetings aren't *that* important, however the people that you're meeting with will slowly begin to trust you less because they'll be conditioned to believe that you don't put a high level of importance on *their* time. The second reason to plan to be twenty minutes early is that sometimes, unforeseen things happen. The parking lot might be full. You might hit traffic. You might have to use the restroom at the last minute. It's wise to give yourself some buffer time to compensate for the unseen. The point is, if you plan to show up twenty minutes prior to your meeting, you'll rarely be late if something unforeseen happens, and you won't be rushing to get there, which allows you to mentally prepare for peak performance," The Icon said.

Perhaps that's why The Icon always exuded such a high level of *relaxed confidence*. He was always over-prepared and was never frantically rushed.

I, being on the other end of the spectrum, always felt under-prepared and was always frantically rushing.

I realized The Icon would teach me many valuable lessons – simple, yet powerful changes I desperately needed to make – that would change my entire approach to business and to life in general.

"It's an easy thing to do, and ultimately, it'll set you apart from everyone else. Develop the habit of showing up early. And you can never be overdressed either, which is why I wanted you to meet me here. I want to introduce you to someone," he said.

In walked an impeccably dressed Italian gentleman, with a measuring tape draped around his neck. The Icon proceeded to introduce us saying, "Vincent, I'd like you to meet Massimo. He's my master tailor. I just flew him in from Milan last night."

"Nice to meet you," I said, standing up to shake his hand.

Massimo didn't speak much English. He was a quiet man, yet pensive. He looked like he was always thinking. Designing. Plotting.

He motioned me to move over in front of a three-way mirror, and looked at me up and down, from several angles. Then, all of a sudden, he started measuring me, taking scrupulous notes on his iPad.

"Kid, we're gonna get you into a proper suit," The Icon said, as he looked at me up and down in the three-way mirror.

I didn't know how to respond. I definitely didn't have the money to afford anything of this caliber. As I looked at The Icon like a deer in the headlights, he started laughing and said, "Don't worry about the price, kid. This one's on me."

Again, I didn't know how to respond.

"Umm… sir, umm… That's incredibly generous of you, but I… umm… I… I can't accept this," I stammered.

"Vincent, it's time you embraced *Rule Number Six: Accepting help doesn't make you any less of a man,*" he told me.

"I appreciate the offer, sir. I really do. It's just that I was taught to never accept a hand out," I explained.

"Vincent, listen. I respect the fact that you want to make it on your own. That's a really admirable quality – one of the qualities I like about you – and that's why I'm doing this for you… because I know you appreciate it," The Icon replied.

I didn't know what to say. So I said the only thing that made me feel just a tad more comfortable, and negotiated, "Okay, how about this… when my business picks up, I'll pay you back."

"Kid, don't worry about it. This is something I want to do for you, and it'll get the ball rolling in the right direction," he reassured me.

Massimo continued to take my measurements, as I continued to wonder why The Icon was so generous towards me, at first with his time, and then with his money. I was a nobody.

What did he see in me?

And why did he want to help me?

Whatever the case was, I was grateful.

So I asked The Icon, "So how does this work? Do I pick out the fabric and the design? I saw this one suit at the mall that was really…"

The Icon cut me off.

"Vincent, do you like sushi?" The Icon inquired.

"Sure," I said.

"Have you ever heard of *Omakase style*?" he asked.

"Oma-what?" I embarrassingly replied.

"*Omakase style* is when you sit down at a sushi bar and let the chef serve you whatever he thinks is best. You essentially relinquish all control, and let the master do his work," he explained.

"So, you don't have ANY say in what you order?" I asked.

"No. When you eat Omakase style, you trust that the sushi chef knows best. In fact, my favorite sushi restaurant is a small, obscure place in Orange County, run by a husband, wife and son. The husband sent his son to train in Japan for four years before he allowed him to work by his side. And you ONLY eat Omakase style there. I took a very successful friend of mine there, and he loved it so much, he went back with his wife the next weekend and he tried to order what he wanted. The Chef threw him out and banned him from the restaurant," The Icon said with a smirk.

He continued, "I also know of this top hair stylist in Newport Beach. Here are the conditions if you want this guy to cut your hair. First off, he only cuts women's hair. Secondly, he charges $350 for the haircut, and he has two assistants that hover around you as he's creating his work of art. And thirdly, the client has no say in the type of hairstyle they're going to get. They sit down in his chair, and he decides what's going to look best on the woman, and just like that, he starts creating his masterpiece."

"But with the Omakase sushi master, and the hot-shot hair stylist, don't they lose clients due to how rigid they are," I dumbfoundedly asked.

"Vincent, when you eat Omakase style, prepare to drop about $200 to $400 per person. Why would someone pay that much for dinner? Why would someone pay $350 for a haircut? I mean, it's *just* a haircut!" The Icon exclaimed.

He continued, "But that's the whole point. It's not *just a haircut*. What you're paying for is the design of a visionary. You don't pay $350 to get shorter hair. You pay $350 for a work of art."

"And the $400 sushi guy, what exactly are you paying for? Fresher fish?" I asked.

"The grade of fish is certainly a factor. But it's more than that. A master sushi chef knows how much wasabi should be on each piece. In fact, he won't even give you an extra lump of wasabi in your shoyu dish. He seasons it the way it's *supposed* to be seasoned. But it goes beyond that. A master sushi chef will orchestrate the order in which each fish is served, because based on how oily each fish is, and how your palate tolerates each transition from fish to fish, the chef will decide which fish should be served in what chronological order," The Icon explained.

"That sounds pretty intense," I responded.

"The point is, regardless of the type of business you're in, you have to develop a strong, unwavering, unapologetic brand. And in a business that's artistically based, the artist needs to fully commit to their style, and walk away from business that deviates from their brand. A master sushi chef... a master hair stylist... a fashion house... all must commit to their brand," The Icon elaborated.

And so I figured that in the case of dialing me in with an $8,000 custom suit, it was wise for me to defer to two people. Massimo, who obviously knew how to construct the perfect suit – a truly bespoke suit – perfectly custom tailored to my very imperfect body... and The Icon, who obviously knew what style I should be wearing.

He further explained, "There's a distinct difference between fashion and style. Anyone with money can buy *fashion*, you know, the latest trends and the hottest labels. But to truly have *style*, that's a whole different level. Having style is about being able to pull together a look – an *iconic* look – that takes people's breath away when you walk into a room. That's what my brand is all about. That's why people will drop six grand on an entry-level suit with my company. They know that if they don't like the design of my line, they're wrong."

"Wait a minute. Did you say they START at $6,000? What do they go up to?" I asked.

"$20,000 for our high-end stuff," he said.

As if it wasn't already clear to me, The Icon lived in a world that I didn't belong to... at least not yet. After my fitting was done, The Icon had lunch brought up to the suite.

We sat down to have lunch in the suite's formal dining room. The dining room table was made of a beautiful solid slab of black walnut wood, about four inches thick, highly polished like a *Ferrari* on a showroom floor. The massive slab of wood sat on one clear, solid *Lucite* leg creating the illusion that it was floating.

Around this work of art sat ten black leather *Eames* chairs. I had a knock-off version of this classically designed chair in my apartment that I used as my work chair. I paid $299 for my knock-off version, but the real *Eames* chairs went for $3,500 each.

As we sat among the $35,000 worth of dining room chairs, we talked about the different types of fabric Massimo worked with, and the proper construction of a truly bespoke suit constructed by a master tailor. I never knew there was so much artistic detail in a suit.

He talked about the different conflicting philosophies in regards to how a suit should be designed, talking about the differences between British design, Italian design and French design. It was quite fascinating.

But he spent the majority of the conversation enthusiastically talking about his brand. In the midst of this discussion, it was intoxicating to see someone so enthusiastic and passionate about his company.

And it wasn't just passion about his company. It was passion about design, or more specifically, passion about the details. The way he talked about the type of stitch work Massimo did, and the hidden seam work inside the suit, behind the lining that nobody sees... that got him just as excited as the visible aesthetics of the suit.

"Perhaps nobody sees the inner-workings of Massimo's craftsmanship, but that's not the point. The point is, our clients know it's there, and that's what matters – the quality of the suit's foundation. Every stitch. Every detail. You see, it's not just about the outward appearance that's important to us. It's also about what's inside," The Icon explained.

I could tell he wasn't just talking about suits at this point.

The Icon was more interested in what people did when no one was looking – what a person did behind the scenes – and the integrity that a person had. It seemed as though he was equally as focused on the integrity that his suits had. Perhaps this was a metaphor for how he lived his life.

I asked him about his pavé blue sapphire cufflinks, which looked like they belonged in a glass case, protected by two armed guards. He told me they were a Father's Day gift from his wife.

"Oh my God," I gushed. "If you don't mind me asking, how much were those?"

"Probably about $5,000," he nonchalantly said.

"Holy cow! My car isn't even worth $5,000!" I exclaimed.

The Icon smiled and said, "Well then I guess we need to work on getting you a better car."

When he talked about design and style, the attention to every little detail was borderline obsessive. But that's what made The Icon great.

Excellence.

Excellence in every area of his life, in every little detail.

And then it donned on me. This was only ONE of his companies. He also owned five other companies.

What made my conversation with The Icon so interesting was that despite his incredibly expensive taste, as well as his life of luxury, he didn't come off as being materialistic whatsoever.

Then he asked me a very interesting question. He asked me, "Vincent, tell me, why do you think you want to be successful?"

I looked at him with my signature dumbfounded expression. "Umm, because I hate being broke," I responded.

"And so you think that if you become rich and successful, you'll be happy, or at least happier?" The Icon inquired.

"Well yeah. I mean, isn't that the whole point?" I asked.

"Vincent, you've just uncovered the primary reason why you're not more successful. You're chasing the money, and the money – in and of itself – won't make you happy. Sure it makes a lot of things easier in life, and sure we all enjoy the finer things in life… but the REAL prize is the feeling of accomplishment you'll have inside. You've got to care more about pursuing excellence than pursuing money, because what you'll learn is that when you do, the money will follow," The Icon explained.

The concept of pursuing excellence was something I'd never heard of before, or even thought about before. Pursuing excellence for the sake of pursuing excellence… it really made me think about what was truly important in life.

It became apparent to me that The Icon's entire life had been built on a set of principles, and this was one of them.

I never really looked at my life from this perspective. Actually, I've never really taken the time to look at my life, or what I stood for, or what would even really make me happy.

As I came to this realization, it was both depressing and enlightening at the same time.

Apparently, The Icon could read my mind, because as I processed all of these realizations, it was like he knew *what* I was realizing, *as* I was realizing it.

And then he made me an offer.

He said, "Vincent, I'm not saying that your vitamin business isn't a good business."

"I know you're not saying that, sir," I interjected. "*I'm* the one saying that."

The Icon burst into laughter. "Okay, fair enough," he said as he struggled to stop laughing.

"Vincent, here's my offer. Not only am I prepared to take you on as my mentee, but I'm also willing to offer you a career opportunity. You'd start off as an intern, which isn't very glamorous in the beginning. It would be a lot of grunt work. A full-time, unpaid internship means you'd probably have to work a side job to pay your bills... but this is the only way you're going to learn what it takes to be successful," he said.

The Icon continued, "Now, I have a side job lined up for you too. I own this hotel we're in right now, *The Hotel 100*, and so you'd intern at my wealth management firm during the day from 7:00 a.m. - 7:00 p.m., then you'd work here at the hotel from 8:00 p.m. - 11:00 p.m. Monday through Friday for $10 an hour, and on Saturdays and Sundays, you'd work here from 7:00 a.m. - 4:00 p.m."

The Icon told me he owned *The Hotel 100* the way a man would tell you that he owns the shoes on his feet... nonchalantly, and matter-of-factly, as if it was an obvious assumption.

He explained to me, "I'm prepared to groom you for bigger and better things, but first, you've got to learn the fundamentals. It would be more hours than you've probably ever worked in your life, so I need to know if you're willing to work this hard. So, are you in or are you out?"

Without hesitation, I exclaimed, "I'm in! Sir, thank you SO much for this opportunity. I promise, I won't let you down. I'll work as many hours as it takes."

"Vincent," he said. "I know all of this sounds very exciting, but you must understand something. I believe you have what it takes to become great, but that potential is meaningless without 100% of your very best effort."

"Sir, I promise you, I'll do whatever it takes," I said, but before I could finish my sentence, he cut me off.

"Vincent," he said. "I don't want to hear it. I don't want you to *tell* me. I just want you to *show* me. You give me 100% of your very best effort, and I'll make you a superstar... but at any moment, if I feel I'm wasting my time with someone that won't give it EVERYTHING they've got, I'm done. Understand?"

"Yes sir. I understand," I said. As much as I wanted to reassure him with my words, I knew he didn't care about *words*. What he cared about was *action*. I promised myself that I would go above and beyond anything he asked me to do, just as Andrei had done.

Then The Icon said, "Vincent, tomorrow will be the first day of the rest of your life. You're going to intern with Joseph, my right-hand man at the firm. Just be at this address tomorrow morning at 7:00 a.m."

The Icon handed me his business card, one of six I was sure. This one was his wealth management firm.

After meeting Andrei, I assumed Joseph was another one of his former protégés, and I eagerly anticipated meeting him.

As I left the hotel, I realized that The Icon didn't make these kind of offers to just *anyone*. As Andrei told me, The Icon had *chosen me*, and that alone gave me hope.

Chapter Five
Elevators

At 6:17 a.m., I promptly pulled into the parking lot of Joseph's office for my 7:00 a.m. meeting with him.

As I walked into this high-rise office building, the lobby exuded wealth. White marble floors. Huge glass doors. Vaulted ceilings. White leather furniture.

This was the big time.

I rode the elevator up to the top floor. When the doors opened, I expected to see a vacant office due to it only being 6:34 a.m.

Instead, I felt like I was walking into a crowded nightclub. Hip-hop music was pumping at a volume level so loud, it seemed almost inappropriate. There were about fifty people meeting inside a huge glass conference room – a conference room that looked like something you'd see in a *Mission Impossible* movie – and they were all dressed like mini-Icons.

Then out of the pack of mini-Icons appeared a massive guy that looked like he was half-bodybuilder, half-billionaire. He had the same aura that Andrei had. Confident. Powerful. Successful.

He walked up to me and said, "You must be Vincent. I'm Joseph. Come on back to my office," as he shook my hand with his Kung Fu grip. His handshake practically cut off the circulation to my arm.

We walked back to Joseph's massive office – a corner office that had a magnificent panoramic view of the city. This was the most impressive office I'd ever seen.

"So you're the kid, huh? I've heard some things about you. Good things," Joseph said as he smiled and chuckled gregariously, inviting me to sit down at his desk with him.

He had this jovial way about him, like he was bulletproof, without a care in the world. Unlike Andrei, Joseph was very easy going. He seemed much more approachable and was certainly less abrasive. I knew Joseph had a story, and I was dying to hear it.

"So how did you meet The Icon?" I asked.

Joseph replied, "About sixteen years ago, I was a cocky, 22-year old kid, right out of college. I wanted to be a Financial Analyst and get into the Hedge Fund business, but at the time, I literally couldn't get a job. I was sending out resumes like crazy, but no one would hire me, so I got into the Financial Advising game on straight commission. My dad wanted to kill me because he didn't believe very many people made it in this business, and quite frankly, he was right."

"How many people DO make it in your line of work?" I asked.

"Less than 3%. But you see, I don't represent the 97%. I'm part of the 3%... the TOP of the 3%," he explained.

He continued, "When I got in this game, I was naïve and thought I knew it all. The first year in this business, I made $188,000, which is a lot for a rookie 22-year old kid. In my second year, I made over $212,000. But then my third year hit, and I barely made a dime."

"If you don't mind me asking, what happened in your third year?" I respectfully inquired.

Joseph said, "I became a member of the *NFL*, which is an acronym for *No Friends Left*. You see, in this business, most people start off their career by hitting up people they know – friends and family – and they try to convert them into clients. Well, my father was a very successful businessman, and so he connected me with some of his rich business associates, which is why I did well in my first couple of years... but after my second year, I extinguished all of his contacts, and I didn't know how to get more clients. That's what typically happens in this business, which is why the turnover rate is so high."

He explained, "Sometimes I think it was a curse to do so well in the first two years of my career. I got spoiled, thinking that I could just keep repeating my good luck... but after two years, my good luck ran out. So there I was, with a major league car payment... a VIP lifestyle... and no income to back it up. I exhausted all of my savings, and I was broke. I felt like I was letting everyone down, especially my wife. It was a very humbling experience. And that's when I met The Icon."

"Let me guess... in a coffee shop, right?" I confidently guessed.

"No, I actually stalked him," he said, mildly chuckling to himself. "I heard about this incredibly successful entrepreneur that was supposed to have the *Magic Touch* when it came to developing businesses, including a wealth management firm. He had reached legendary status in this industry, and had built his firm using a completely unorthodox business model. The Icon had developed a marketing system that could generate high net worth clients right out of thin air. No one had ever done what he had done. He had literally revolutionized the financial industry, and I wanted *in*."

Joseph continued, "So I swallowed my pride, and tried to get an interview with him. I called his office everyday for 26 days straight, but his assistant kept telling me that he wasn't hiring. So I decided to walk into his office unannounced, with a $300 bottle of añejo tequila – which is his favorite by the way – and waited in his foyer for three hours. I knew he'd have to come out at some point, at least to use the restroom or go to lunch."

Just hearing Joseph talk about his creative way of getting The Icon's attention made me feel that much more fortunate that he had chosen me. Joseph had to practically stalk The Icon for a chance to interview with him, while I on the other hand, seemed to have lucked out. It made me appreciate this opportunity even more.

Joseph continued, "So at 12:31 p.m., The Icon walked right by me on his way to lunch. I jumped up and followed him into the elevator. I knew I only had about 20 seconds to introduce myself, so I was talking a mile-a-minute about how I had called his office for 26 days in a row, begging for an interview. I handed him the $300 bottle of tequila, and begged him for the chance to interview with him."

Joseph smiled as he recalled his *Icon-stalking* incident, saying, "I begged him to allow me to take him to lunch that day… he accepted… and the rest is history. I think my tenacity impressed him the most. That was fourteen years ago. Today, I'm 38-years old, and I run the entire firm… his firm. After proving myself to him for over 10 years, he believed in me so much, he made me a partner, so technically, this is *our* firm."

"Wow, you own part of this firm?" I asked.

"Yeah. Crazy, huh? We should do a little over $350 million in insurance premiums this year, and have over $23 billion in assets under management," said Joseph.

"Wow! That's some serious cheddar. Umm, can I ask you something personal?" I sheepishly asked.

"Sure. I can't promise you that I'll answer your question, but sure, you can ask," he said with a smile.

"The Icon told me that one of my problems is that I've been too focused on chasing the money, as opposed to pursuing excellence. But I see guys like you and Andrei… I'm assuming you know Andrei, right?" I asked.

"Of course. Andrei runs The Icon's custom jewelry company," Joseph confirmed.

"Yeah, well, I look at you and Andrei, and it's obvious you guys are making a ton of money – probably more than most professional athletes – and it's hard for me to believe you guys aren't in it for the money," I confessed.

"I appreciate your honesty. Now I know why The Icon likes you. The reality is that in the beginning, it WAS all about the money for me. The Icon told me the same thing about pursuing excellence, and how the feeling of pride would be more valuable than the money. I listened, but I didn't *get it* right away," Joseph explained.

He continued, "The Icon was always talking to me about the importance of living a life of *significance,* and how I would never be great until I focused more on impacting other people's lives instead of just impacting my own bank account. It took me years to figure out what he was trying to teach me."

It was obvious that Joseph understood the bigger picture of The Icon's vision, which was to impact other people's lives. I would later learn that this was the most important thing in The Icon's life. It was his personal mission.

Joseph stood up and motioned me to follow him. As we walked over to the other side of his enormous office, Joseph explained to me, "One day, The Icon sent me a letter that changed my life. That's it hanging on my wall right there in those three frames. Let me read it to you," Joseph said as we walked up to them.

Joseph,

Have you ever had a recurring dream? The same dream theme, played out in countless scenarios... perhaps even since childhood?

Maybe it's the one where your teeth are all falling out, or you end up finding yourself naked in public.

Well, ever since I was a kid, I had dreams about elevators. Actually, they were nightmares. I would step into an elevator, and all of a sudden, I'd find myself standing on a tiny little pedestal, looking down the elevator shaft, afraid to fall hundreds of feet to my demise.

Sometimes, the nightmare would take place in a high-rise office building. Sometimes, it would take place in a futuristic space station.

These nightmares would take place in all different kinds of places, but the one theme they all had in common was fear. I was afraid that I would lose my balance and fall down the elevator shaft and die.

The last time I remember having one of these nightmares, I was in a 50-floor high-rise building. The elevator was made of glass, and it went far beyond the 50th floor. It kept going and going and going... higher and higher and higher, up into the clouds.

When I reached the top floor, it was a very expensive restaurant... kind of like a private, members-only club. I was so high up in the sky in this glass elevator, that I could see everything, like I was on top of the world. I remember lying down on the elevator floor, so petrified of the height, fearing that I would fall right out of the sky.

I must admit, I'm rather fascinated with the psychological aspect of dreams in general, but more specifically, recurring dreams. What is the origin of a dream? What makes some of them seem so vivid and real? What do they mean?

I believe that every dream we have, originates deep in our subconscious mind. Our worries, fears and insecurities surface in our dreams in many different ways... sometimes in the most bizarre story lines.

If I was to psycho-analyze my elevator nightmares, I would say that the fear of falling down these elevator shafts in my nightmares stemmed from my fear of failure... the fear of beginning to rise to new heights and falling/failing in the process.

So the question is, why elevators?

I believe the elevators were symbolic of my opportunity to rise to new levels... levels that I had never reached before... and that deep down, perhaps I felt unprepared... and more specifically, unworthy.

You see, we as human beings are all insecure to a certain degree. We all know that we have shortcomings in different areas, and we tend to be afraid that once other people are made aware of our imperfections, that they'll reject us. And so as a defense mechanism, many people attempt to put on a front and try to impress people with an image that they think the other person wants to see.

Basically, people lie and posture their way into a façade, hoping that other people never discover their inadequacies.

But there is also an opposite, counterintuitive defense mechanism... one that makes no logical sense whatsoever... but I would have to say the large majority of people involuntarily resort to it... which is the curse of self-sabotage.

Self-sabotage happens when a person is heading down the right path... they're making noteworthy progress... but right when they're about to succeed, they do something stupid to screw it up. It's not that the person is lazy, or unfocused, or literally stupid.

What's happening is that deep down, the person doesn't truly believe that they're worthy of success, and so they'll do something brain-dead to sabotage their own success.

This phenomenon happens because of the person having low self-esteem and a low self-concept. So what does this have to do with my dreams about elevators?

Well, I believe that God only grants us massive success when we truly feel that we are deserving of it. If we don't feel that we've done everything we could... if we feel like we didn't truly give it 100% of our effort... or if we don't feel good enough about ourselves... then we don't truly expect success to flow.

In the early years of my career, I didn't have the same conviction and confidence in myself that I do now... not even close. I knew that I had worked hard, and I was more confident than most people, but I didn't have the swagger that I have today.

The connection between what I'm sharing with you, and my recurring elevator nightmares is pretty obvious. I was afraid of where the elevator was taking me because I didn't believe in myself enough. I almost feel like God was trying to tell me that He was going to take me to a new level that I didn't even know existed, but my fear of falling kept me from just enjoying the elevator ride.

The last time I had one of my elevator nightmares was right before my daughter was born. Maybe it was the fear of the unknown, and that fatherhood would challenge me. Maybe it was trying to figure out what my next move in business would be.

The point is, I don't have these nightmares anymore. I am at a place today that is more confident... more at peace... more appreciative... more adamant about my vision... more energized... more focused... more motivated... and more powerful than I have ever been in, ever.

It's one thing to BE strong. It's another thing to KNOW that you're strong.

It's one thing to BE healed... but it's another thing to KNOW that you're healed.

It's one thing to BE prepared... but it's another thing to KNOW that you're prepared.

It's one thing to BE blessed... but it's another thing to KNOW that you're blessed.

It's one thing to BE worthy... but it's another thing to KNOW that you're worthy.

Yes, you have to work hard... grind it out... pay your dues... work harder when you're tired... work smarter when you're frustrated... regain focus when you're overwhelmed... but above all, you have to remember that you're part of my organization for a reason.

Joseph, you didn't end up here by mistake.

Think about everything that had to happen for you to end up here today. What if you hadn't ever heard of me... or if you hadn't had the guts to walk into my office with that bottle of tequila... or you gave up after the 22nd attempt to get an interview... or if you had listened to your stupid friend that told you not to take a commission-only position.

You are here because you've been afforded a unique opportunity that most people never experience... the opportunity to truly make something of yourself that you can be proud of. And so what does that mean?

What it means is that you were chosen to be here, before I even chose you to be here. This is your destiny.

Don't let the heights of the elevator scare you. Embrace these heights that are in your near future.

And always remember that the elevator wouldn't have stopped at your floor to pick you up if you weren't meant to step in and go up.

-The Icon

I could see that reading this letter moved Joseph's soul, the way a beautiful song or deep poem moves you at the cellular level.

The Icon had that effect on people.

It seemed as though everyone he touched in his life was somehow changed forever. I hoped it would be this way for me too. In a very ironic way, having only met him three times, he had already begun to change my life forever.

Then Joseph said, "So did The Icon tell you what your first internship assignment is yet?"

"No, he didn't," I responded.

"Okay," Joseph said laughing. "You're going to intern with me, here at the firm, learning how to do what we do here... wealth management, which includes investments, hedge funds, life insurance, and a whole array of different financial instruments. You're going to work harder than you ever have, but you're going to learn a lot... probably a lot more than you bargained for."

"I'm ready!" I exclaimed. "Oh, Joseph. One quick question. The Icon told me to ask you about *Rule Number Seven.*"

Joseph smiled and said, "*Rule Number Seven* is what The Icon was teaching me in that letter I just read to you. You see, my problem back then was that I had all the tools to become successful, except for one. I didn't believe in myself. Not because I didn't think I was smart or capable, but because I just never thought I deserved it. I used to believe that some people in this world have good luck, and others just don't... and I started to believe that I was one of the ones that didn't. I can't really explain why I had this fear – this doubt – but I'd look at these super successful people that I aspired to be like, and deep down, I doubted my self-worth. That's when The Icon taught me *Rule Number Seven: Never Sell Yourself Short.*"

I studied Joseph as he spoke to me. Behind his kind eyes was an overwhelming sense of gratitude. I could tell that he appreciated what he had, and that he was incredibly grateful for what The Icon had taught him, and for his relationship with The Icon.

Similar to my interaction with Andrei, I saw the life-changing affect that one man could have on another man's life. And I also understood why these two guys were willing to spend their time meeting with me.

It was because The Icon took the time to spend with them. They felt an obligation to The Icon, but they also felt an obligation to give back to the universe what had been given to them: *Opportunity.*

Great opportunities rarely come along – maybe once in a lifetime – and for some people, they never come along. Andrei and Joseph were two people that were blessed with great opportunities, and they capitalized on them. I hoped to join them in this exclusive club they were part of.

Joseph walked me out onto the sales floor, where I saw Junior Financial Advisors that had just started with the firm, as well as the *Big Dogs* that had been at the firm for several years making the big bucks. Some of these Senior Financial Advisors were making over $700,000 a year, which seemed almost too good to be true… until I got a taste of what they had to do to get there.

These guys paid a lot of dues to elevate their careers to where they were. As I watched the action on the floor and talked to Joseph, asking him a zillion questions, I learned that every Senior Advisor started out as a Junior Advisor. They had all earned their stripes as Junior Advisors, which entailed a lot of grunt work.

Tons of cold calling, and tons of rejection.

These guys were making over 400 phone dials per day. I watched the sales floor for the first half of my day, scrupulously taking notes on all of my observations. I knew that both Joseph and The Icon would test me at some point to see how much I was soaking in from the experience, and I wanted to be over-prepared, which went back to *Rule Number Two: Don't ever let your brain be lazy. When someone asks you a question, think about it thoroughly.*

I wanted to be sure that when they asked me what I had learned on my first day, that I would have already thought about it thoroughly, and that I'd be prepared to intelligently and thoroughly articulate my observations.

I noticed some of these guys actually made a game out of it. Every time one of them booked an appointment with a prospective client, they dropped down to the ground, pumped out twenty push ups, rang a cow bell that hung on the wall, and high-fived each other like they had just hit a homerun.

They seemed to actually *enjoy* the challenge.

But there was another group of Junior Advisors that didn't seem to have the same vigor. They moved a little slower, talked a little softer, and didn't look like they enjoyed their work as much as the other group.

I wondered why.

I also listened to some of the conversations the Senior Advisors were having with the Junior Advisors about their technique and voice intonation on the phone. It was like they were psychology professors, talking about the subconscious mind and how the prospective clients would interpolate the message they were delivering.

I never knew there was that much science in selling, which was probably why I wasn't very successful in my own sales career.

Just before 12:00 p.m., Joseph walked up to me and suggested we go to lunch and debrief. I was so fascinated with what I was witnessing on the sales floor that I didn't want to leave, but Joseph insisted.

As we sat down for lunch, Joseph asked me the question that I knew was coming. He asked, "So Vincent, what'd you learn watching the action on the floor this morning?"

Prepared, I took out my notepad and went bullet point by bullet point down the list of notes I had taken. However, there was one particular observation I was the most curious about.

I asked him, "Why are some of your guys so fired up, and... well, I hope you don't take offense to this... but some of them look like they don't even want to be here?"

"You noticed that, huh?" Joseph said, chuckling as if he knew exactly what I was alluding to. He continued, "That's the difference between the ones that will become millionaires and the ones that will wash out. That was the difference between me and the other 97% of the guys that quit and failed."

"So why are those other guys even here if they don't like what they do?" I asked.

"I know it looks like they don't want to be here, and maybe they don't, but there's something inside of them that wants to achieve greatness. You see, these guys – every one of these guys – are working on straight commission with no base salary. And the reason they're willing to do this is that they want more out of life than a cubicle job and a cruddy paycheck. They're trying to grind it out and make it to the big time, but they're missing the boat… and the boat they're missing is that THIS is the best time of their career. That's what they don't get," Joseph said, as he became more and more enthusiastic.

I countered, "What do you mean this is the best time of their career?

"Vincent, if you can grasp what I'm about to tell you – I mean REALLY grasp it – you've got a shot at massive success. This is the key to success, especially in the beginning of your career, and if you never embrace this, you'll most likely give up and quit. This is *Rule Number Eight: The Beginning Days Of Your Career Will One Day Be Your Good Ole Days,*" Joseph said.

I almost said, "Huh?" but fortunately, I stopped myself, remembering Andrei's words. Instead, I replied, "Could you elaborate on *Rule Number Eight* for me?"

"Sure," Joseph said, looking pleased that I was so intrigued. He shared with me, "Vincent, I learned *Rule Number Eight* the hard way. In fact, I'm one of the few people I know that succeeded at this firm without ever mastering *Rule Number Eight*. I didn't fully learn the essence of this rule until I became successful, and by that time, it was too late to put it into practice. But when I look back over the course of my career, I realize that I almost didn't make it here because of this."

He continued, "I was always so angry at myself for not being further along in my career than I thought I should have been. I was incredibly hard on myself – too hard on myself – and that perpetual dissatisfaction with myself was destructive. I was angry and ashamed of not being where I thought I should be, when I thought I should be there. I felt like I was letting myself down, and even worse, I thought I was letting The Icon down. He tried teaching me *Rule Number Eight* so many times, but I just refused to listen to him. It's a miracle he didn't fire me back then."

I could see Joseph beginning to get sentimental as these words left his lips. Joseph was one of those guys that was so comfortable in his own skin that he could be totally transparent with his emotions.

He didn't fear judgment whatsoever.

It's not that he didn't care what people thought about him – he was very consciously aware of how others perceived him – but as long as they knew where he truly stood, he didn't care if they agreed with him or not. He had a *raw* kind of confidence about him, and he wore his heart on his sleeve.

I proceeded to ask, "Why do you say it's a miracle The Icon didn't fire you back then?"

"If you could have seen me back then, you'd understand. I was emotionally volatile back then, and I was relentless about pursuing success. The Icon knew that I would do anything he asked me to do, just to prove my loyalty to him."

Joseph continued, "One time, we were in a crowded restaurant, and he accidently bumped into a guy – a big guy – and the dude got up in The Icon's face, ready to throw blows. I jumped in and put the guy in a chokehold, wrestling him down to the floor. It took three security guards to pry me off that guy. The Icon scolded me, saying how stupid of a move that was, but I could tell he kind of liked it too."

"The Icon LOVES loyalty," Joseph explained, smiling as he reminisced about strong-arming the guy in the restaurant.

"But the anger I'm talking about was more about wanting so badly to be successful, and being embarrassed about not having the money to back it up. I knew my career was going in the right direction once I started working with The Icon, and I knew riches wouldn't come overnight, but I still wanted them to... and it ate away at my ego to not have the material trappings of success yet," Joseph said.

"How long did it take you to start killing it once you met The Icon?" I asked.

"Three years," Joseph said. "And the reality is, it took The Icon longer than three years before he started killing it in his career, so in retrospect, I don't know why I felt so ashamed of not getting off to a faster start. In reality, three years is nothing. Three years is a really fast start compared to most people."

I responded, "Joseph, if I could be a fraction as successful as you are in three years, I'd be in heaven."

Joseph took a moment, staring into my soul. He then said, "Well, let's see how you do with the grunt work first. Then we'll talk about the next step. But I have to tell you a story before we go back to the office. You know what I was saying about *The Good Ole Days*? What I realize now, that I didn't realize then, is that the fondest memories I have regarding my career aren't during the times when my success had already materialized. My fondest memories are all during the beginning stages of my career when I was struggling."

He continued, "So my advice is this... never forget what this feels like... right now. Never forget how nervous you are right now... the feelings of anxiety, worry, and fear. Because one day, when you're a successful leader, you're going to be having the same talk I'm having with you... but the difference is that you're going to be in my position, and you're going to be encouraging a young, new protégé, telling them about your *Good Ole Days*. So if you can remember EXACTLY how you feel right now, your people will be able to relate to you. They'll aspire to be like you, but more importantly, they'll believe that with your guidance, they can be successful too. You need to instill the belief in them that if you did it, then maybe they can do it too."

I thought about what Joseph said.

Essentially, that's what he was doing with me.

Joseph was a sharp guy, no doubt. But the reason he was so successful was due to his relentless effort to prove himself to The Icon, and THAT, I believed I could duplicate. But I still didn't understand why Joseph said that it was a miracle The Icon didn't fire him.

So I inquired, "Joseph, why did you say you almost got fired?"

"Vincent, I wanted so badly to impress everyone back then. Maybe it was because I never felt like I measured up to my father's standards – maybe I was just insecure in general – but I pretty much embellished everything about myself back then. One day, I was talking to one of the new Junior Advisors at the firm. I had only been working there for a year, and I wanted to feel like a big shot. I was doing well, but I was far from being a heavy hitter yet. So I told the kid I was making double what I was actually making... and just as that lie left my lips, The Icon walked up behind me," Joseph recalled.

I could sense Joseph's embarrassment as he confessed to me, but that didn't stop him. He was a strong, formidable man, yet in that moment, I could tell that he was ashamed.

Joseph continued, "The Icon told me to follow him into his office. I totally expected him to ream me right there. He sat me down and asked me why I felt the need to lie about my income, but I think he already knew the reason. That's the thing about The Icon. It's like he knows what's going on in your head without you having to tell him."

I knew exactly what Joseph was talking about. The Icon always seemed all-knowing. The insight he had into everyone's life was uncanny.

Joseph went on and said, "The Icon told me that there's nothing he hates more than a liar... and that's what I was. I was a liar. I never lied about anything that would hurt anyone, but I constantly lied about my track record, or more specifically, my lack thereof. So when he asked me about why I lied about my income to that new Junior Advisor, I confessed to him that I wanted to be seen as the top guy, because deep down, I didn't feel worthy."

When Joseph told me this, I could tell that it hurt him to share this with me, but he was totally transparent with me, nonetheless. I could feel the pain in his voice as he recounted this moment of shame with me, and I could relate. I too felt embarrassed and ashamed that I wasn't more successful at this point in my life, and from Joseph's story, I figured he felt the same during the beginning stages of his career.

And then he reaffirmed what I had already figured out. Joseph said, "The Icon helped me realize, in that moment of getting busted, that I should feel proud that I was putting everything on the line to become successful... that my pride should be based on my effort and commitment to chase my dream, not in my results... and that if I focused on the right things, that the results would naturally come."

This was the same advice The Icon had already given me. There was always a consistency in the lessons he taught people.

Joseph continued, "When he caught me in that lie, I thought for sure that he was going to fire me, because I know how he feels about liars. But instead, he used it as an opportunity to teach me the most valuable lesson I've ever learned, which is *Rule Number Nine: Never Despise The Days Of Small Beginnings*."

And there it was.

The key to resolving my insecurities.

Joseph made me realize that everyone, including him, started off small.

And that was where I was starting off.

Small.

Joseph explained, "The days of small beginnings are absolutely necessary. Sure, they aren't *glamorous* years, but they are *necessary* years. These are the *foundation building* years. Vincent, when you see a high-rise building being built, in the beginning months – for months and months – all you see is a big hole in the ground with a bunch of concrete. It's not very pretty, nor is it glamorous. For months and months, you see this ugly slab of concrete with a bunch of iron rods sticking up out of it. For months and months, it doesn't look like anything is happening – like there's no progress being made – but nothing could be further from the truth. The foundation is being built. Then, all of a sudden, it seems like the entire building – twenty floors – is erected in just a few short weeks. Why is that? It's because it takes much longer to build the foundation than it does to build the twenty floors. That's how the beginning stage of your career is. In the beginning, it feels like you're doing all this work and getting dismal results. It feels like your efforts are in vain. But again, nothing could be further from the truth. A powerful ground swell is building, and soon, the world will see your power. Don't let your ego get the best of you like it got the best of me. As much as you want everyone to acknowledge your success, you've got to be patient during this building stage. You see, your so-called *Small Beginnings* may look small on the surface, but the reality is, you're building the foundation of your empire."

To hear Joseph talk about the necessity of the foundation building years made me feel better about my lack of progress in my life, and I hoped that he would help me begin building my foundation.

Joseph then walked me over to a massive painting that hung on his wall. It was a long, horizontal painting, abstract in its composition, and minimalist in its presentation.

It spanned about eight feet in length, and the canvas's midnight black background had one thick white brush stroke that ran from left to right, curving up at the end.

Joseph said, "The Icon actually painted this himself."

"He's an artist, too?" I asked in bewilderment.

"The Icon is a Renaissance Man. He's unexpectedly artistic for a business mogul, I know. Among his many talents, he's a master in the art of Japanese calligraphy known as *kanji*. He created this painting using a large, traditional Japanese brush made of bamboo called a *fude*. The minimalist art of using a *fude* is not as simple as it looks. A bamboo *fude* is essentially a piece of bamboo whose end is distressed and frayed, creating a rough, irregular brush-like texture. The stroke of this ancient artistic method creates a perfectly imperfect brush stroke," said Joseph.

He continued, "You see, this painting represents a graph. The bottom, horizontally running edge of the painting represents the *time* axis... and the left, vertically running edge of the painting represents the *success* axis. And this brush stroke you see here represents the path of an entrepreneur."

Everything The Icon created was rooted in a life lesson.

"As the brush stroke runs horizontally, from left to right, time is elapsing... but there are no vertical signs of progress. As more and more time elapses, the aspiring entrepreneur's progress continues to flat-line," Joseph explained.

I was certainly familiar with flat-lining in my career.

"Now, you see this little speck right here?" Joseph asked, pointing at a black speck of paint in the middle of the white brush stroke.

"Yeah, is that intentional?" I inquired.

Joseph smiled, knowing that I already knew the answer to that question.

Everything The Icon did was *intentional*.

He explained, "That speck of paint represents the point at which most people quit and give up on their dreams. They've been flat-lining for so long with little or no progress, that they assume success is never going to happen for them, so they give up. But notice, that speck is placed right before the brush stroke starts to curve upwards – right before we start seeing progress – and very shortly thereafter, the brush stroke starts to soar upwards."

As Joseph continued to explain the symbolism of The Icon's painting, I literally got goose bumps. It was like he was prophetically illustrating what I so desperately hoped would happen to me and my career.

He continued, "Vincent, this painting – this graph – tells you everything you need to know about the life of an aspiring entrepreneur. Do you see how the brush stroke takes off vertically so abruptly and so drastically? That's what happens when your business hits critical mass – when it hits that point where everything comes together – and when everything comes together, your success takes off exponentially."

Whether or not Joseph meant to or not, I felt like he was including me in this category.

Again, goose bumps.

Joseph looked deep into my eyes and said, "So Vincent, don't despise these days of small beginnings – these days of flat-lining. Without them, it would be impossible to build your empire – to soar like the brush stroke in this painting – because it would have nothing to stand on. It wouldn't have a solid foundation. Always remember that when you're building your foundation, there may not be any visible signs of progress, but that doesn't mean that progress isn't being made. And right at that moment of maximum frustration – right when most people give up and quit – if you can keep on pushing past that point, that's when everything will turn around for you, and you'll start soaring."

I had always begrudged not being further along in my career, but perhaps this was all part of the process. I mean, Andrei was eating leftovers from people's plates when he met The Icon. Joseph just admitted to me that he felt the need to lie about his lack of income.

And there I was, with no signs of success in my life, yet The Icon was willing to invest his time in me. Andrei took the time to meet with me. And now, Joseph was spilling his guts to me, on the first day of my internship.

What these guys had in common was an undying loyalty to The Icon, but more importantly, it was an undying loyalty to a set of rules – a set of *life principles*.

These rules were like a special code they lived by. They laid out the blueprint for success in life, not just success in business.

Perhaps that's why The Icon seemed so grounded and relaxed in his confidence. He knew who he was and what he stood for, and was unwavering in his resolve.

I knew that this was what I wanted in my own life – not just money – but an inner confidence that I could feel good about. That was the primary gift that The Icon passed on to Andrei and Joseph, and now that gift was being passed on to me.

I was lucky.

It was apparent that I was going to get a lot more out of this experience with The Icon than just a career opportunity.

I was going to learn how to become a better *man*.

As insecure and unaccomplished as I was at that time, Joseph made me feel comfortable being in my own skin. Yes, I still felt like a fish out of water, but the metamorphosis of converting my gills into lungs was being made possible, first by The Icon, and now by Joseph.

This gave me hope.

The rest of the day seemed to fly by, and before I knew it, it was 7:00 p.m. Joseph said, "Alright Vincent, off to your night job at the hotel. I'll see you here tomorrow morning at 7:00 a.m., sharp."

Obviously, I knew that meant 6:40 a.m.

Chapter Six
The Hotel 100

I realized that I only had an hour before my shift at *The Hotel 100*, so I quickly grabbed a $0.99 hamburger at *Jack In The Box*, and rushed off to the hotel.

As I briskly walked into the lobby, I was greeted by Francisco, the head concierge.

"Mr. Vincent. Welcome back. So how was your first day at Mr. Icon's firm?" Francisco inquired.

"It was great. I learned a lot today," I replied.

Francisco smiled and said, "Good. You're about to learn a whole lot more tonight. Come, follow me Mr. Vincent."

I was given a freshly pressed hotel uniform, a nametag, and was introduced to several hotel employees. Based on the level of respect they all gave Francisco, I quickly figured out that he was the boss of the operation... The Icon's eyes and ears of *The Hotel 100*.

As Francisco escorted me back to the main entrance of the hotel, he informed me that I would be greeting guests as they arrived. Not exactly the most interesting job task, but I was grateful for anything to help me pay the bills while I interned with Joseph at the firm.

As a guest walked through the main entrance held open by the doorman, Francisco greeted the guest with a warm smile and said, "Welcome back, sir. Chilled bottle of water... compliments of *The Hotel 100*," as he presented an ice cold bottle of water to the gentleman as if it were an *Oscar* award.

Francisco explained to me that I'd be greeting guests in the same fashion. Pretty simple.

Just as another car pulled up to the main entrance, Francisco instructed me to get ready and said, "You're up Mr. Vincent."

A well-dressed gentleman walked in and immediately gave Francisco a friendly nod. Clearly, he was a regular. I stepped up and said, "Welcome to *The Hotel 100*, sir. Would you like a bottle of water?"

He accepted the bottle of water, smiled at Francisco, and said, "Who's the new kid?"

"This is Mr. Vincent. It's his first night on the job, so he's learning how we operate," Francisco said, in an almost apologetic tone.

"Not a problem," said the gentleman, as he looked at me with a warm smile, and said, "Son, you're learning from the best."

It was like they were speaking in code, and I didn't know what was going on. I sort of felt like there was a joke in progress, and that I was the butt of the joke.

And so I asked Francisco, "Did I do something wrong?"

Francisco responded with an empathetic smile and said, "You didn't do anything necessarily wrong, however let me explain how our employees are trained here at *The Hotel 100*. Mr. Icon is very specific about how he wants us to communicate with our guests. For example, when we greet a guest, unless they're checking in for the first time, we always say, *'Welcome back,'* because it subconsciously implies that they're coming back home. We want them to feel like *The Hotel 100* is their second home, not just a hotel."

"Okay, interesting. Got it," I said in an all-knowing tone of voice, as if that one tip had taught me everything I needed to know.

Boy, was I wrong.

Francisco continued, "That's not it Mr. Vincent. When you present the bottle of water to a guest, you must say *'chilled bottle of water.'* It sounds more refreshing, and when a guest returns from being out all day, they're coming back home to relax, unwind, and cool down. A *chilled* bottle of water implies that we *prepared* the bottle just for them."

Something told me that Francisco wasn't done yet. He was just getting started.

"And that's not all Mr. Vincent. It needs to be said as a statement, not a question. We say, *'Chilled bottle of water.'* We don't ask them if they'd like one. We present the bottle to them as a gift. We also say, *'Compliments of The Hotel 100'* which subconsciously reminds them that it IS a gift, eliciting a *'Thank You'* from the guest. Every interaction we have with a guest should elicit a *'Thank You.'* This is important because it does two things. One, it makes our guests feel like they're being taken care of. And two, when a guest says, *'Thank You,'* who hears it?" Francisco asked.

"We hear it," I responded.

"That's pretty obvious. But who else hears it?" Francisco prodded.

I thought for a moment, and then responded, "The other guests hear it too."

"Exactly. When guests hear other guests thank our staff, it creates an environment of gratitude and appreciation. It's much more powerful for a guest to witness the gratitude and satisfaction of another guest's experience with us, than it is to show them any award we may have won, or any rating we may have received. It's a real-life, real-time testimonial," Francisco explained.

The more I heard Francisco talk about the psychology behind something that I thought was so simple, the more I realized that The Icon's diabolical approach to every little detail of his businesses was applied to EVERYTHING.

To think there was a psychological communication strategy applied to handing a hotel guest a bottle of water. It made me even more intrigued by what I was going to learn through this experience... not only interning with Joseph at the firm, but also working with Francisco at the hotel.

Andrei and Joseph had such interesting stories and histories with The Icon, and based on how deeply entrenched Francisco was in The Icon's business, I assumed he had an equally interesting history with him as well.

I assumed correctly.

Towards the end of my shift, Francisco escorted me into his private office to wrap up the evening. He had a warmth and wisdom that came from being an old soul.

I asked Francisco about how he met The Icon. I knew it would be an interesting story, but I had no idea just how interesting it would be.

Francisco told me, "I'm originally from Nicaragua. I grew up in Majagual, a small village with no running water. In fact, when I was a young boy, my job was to carry buckets of water from the well back to our small home. We were very poor. We lived in a two-room house... our walls were made of cinder blocks and cement... and our roof was made of scraps of corrugated sheet metal. My parents slept in one room, and I shared the other room with my two younger brothers and younger sister, sleeping on a concrete floor. We didn't have much in terms of money, but we were happy because we had each other."

Francisco paused, and gazed off into the distance. I could tell he was debating on whether or not to tell me something very personal.

And then he continued, "When I was 15-years old, my parents were murdered. Some local thieves broke into our home and were going to rob my parents at gunpoint, but when the robbers realized that my parents didn't have any money, they shot them in cold blood. I woke up in the middle of the night when I heard the gunshots, and I ran into their room. My mother was shot in the head, and was obviously already dead. But my father was shot in the chest, and was still alive. He must have known he was about to die, because as I held his head, he whispered to me, *'Francisco, promise me you'll take care of your brothers and sister. You're the man of the house now.'* And when I nodded my head, making that promise, he smiled, and passed away in my arms right there."

I could feel the pain in Francisco's voice, and I could see the pain on his face.

It reminded me of a Smokey Robinson song, where the lyrics say, *"Take a good look at my face / You'll see my smile looks out of place / If you look closer, it's easy to trace / The tracks of my tears."*

I could tell Francisco had a rough life growing up. He went on to tell me that from that moment on, at only fifteen years of age, it was his responsibility to take care of his brothers and sister.

I couldn't imagine what that must have been like for him.

He recounted, "Some of the people in our village helped me look after my siblings, making sure we had food. There was a family that lived close by that helped watch my 7-year old brother and 5-year old sister during the day, while I went to work with my 12-year old brother. There was a resort in a town called *San Juan del Sur*. My brother and I were selling necklaces and bracelets to tourists in the hotel, without the hotel's permission... and eventually, we got caught. The hotel manager was in the process of calling the police, when one of the guests walked up and pulled the hotel manager aside. After about five minutes, the hotel manager walked up to me and said, *'You're lucky,'* and walked away. The hotel guest approached me and my brother, and sat us down."

I interjected, "Let me guess. It was The Icon."

Francisco smiled, and I could tell by his smile that I had guessed correctly.

"Mr. Icon sat me and my brother down and asked, *'Who do you work for?'* I was so scared of him," Francisco said. "I told him that I worked for myself, and that was the truth. I'd buy these necklaces and bracelets, and sell them to tourists, and that's how I supported myself and my brothers and sister. I taught my 12-year old brother how to do it too. He was my wingman. He was too young to work, but we did what we had to do in order to survive. We were a good team."

I then asked Francisco, "So what happened next?"

He replied, "Mr. Icon was a young, aspiring businessman who was planning to open a luxury boutique resort in *San Juan del*

Sur, not far from the resort where we first met. He called it *El Cien*, which translated from Spanish to English, meant *"The 100."* And he made me an offer I couldn't refuse."

I inquired, "So what was the offer?"

Francisco's lips started to quiver. I could tell he was getting very emotional retelling his story to me.

"Mr. Icon hired me and my brother to work at his hotel, and paid us more than double what we were making selling necklaces and bracelets. He was single at the time, and he worked seven days a week, all day, and practically all night. And so did I. My brother and I worked by his side, all day, and at the end of the day, I sent my brother home to watch our other siblings... but I stayed behind, working right along side Mr. Icon. I was his right-hand man. Imagine that... a 15-year old kid, following him around all day and all night," Francisco said.

I then asked him, "So how did you get here to the United States?"

He said, "Mr. Icon built *El Cien* from nothing into being the premier luxury resort in *San Juan del Sur*, and really, the premier resort in all of Nicaragua. It took him three years to do it, and by that time, A-List celebrities were clamoring to stay with us... and right at the three-year mark, he sold it. He made millions. This was Mr. Icon's first big success in business. His plan was to move back to The United States and open a new hotel in Beverly Hills... *The Hotel 100*... and he asked me to come with him."

"But what about your brothers and sister?" I asked.

Francisco looked away. I could tell there was a story behind this story, but I had no idea what I was about to uncover. As Francisco's eyes reconnected with mine, his lips began to quiver again.

"I was 18-years old when Mr. Icon made me that offer. He told me that he could hire me on a work Visa, which authorized me to work here in the states. But my brothers and sister were too young to qualify, and the only way for my brothers and sister to come with me was for them to become American citizens... and the only way for them to become American citizens, was for them to be adopted by an American," said Francisco.

"So what did you do?" I inquired.

"I already knew the laws, and so when Mr. Icon offered me that opportunity, I knew I had to turn it down. My primary job was to take care of my siblings. And just as I was about to tell him that I couldn't leave my family behind, he told me what he had done," Francisco said.

He continued, "Mr. Icon asked me for my permission to adopt my brothers and sister, because he knew this was the only way to keep my family together. He took us all in as his own. Mr. Icon put all of my siblings through private school. He hired a full-time nanny to help raise them. Mr. Icon was only 31 years old when he took us in. He literally became our father."

I could feel the magnitude of Francisco's gratitude towards The Icon. His life, and his family's life, had been changed forever.

I did the math in my head, quickly recounting Francisco's incredible life story, and calculated that The Icon was only 28-years old when he met the 15-year old Francisco in *San Juan del Sur*, Nicaragua.

Francisco went on to tell me that it had been 31 years ago that he met The Icon, which would make Francisco 49-years old today, which would put The Icon at 62-years old today.

Wow.

The Icon was in such good shape that from his appearance, you'd think he was ten years younger. But from his level of success, you'd think he was twenty years older.

What I already knew continued to be reinforced. The Icon had the ability to transform people's lives. Everyone he touched in his life had been so greatly impacted by him, that he had built a legacy that extended far beyond monetary rewards.

Francisco continued, "Mr. Icon not only gave me a job, he taught me valuable lessons in business and in life. When he opened *The Hotel 100*, this hotel we're in right now, he told me that he wanted me to learn every little detail of how to run the business. It was an opportunity that no one would have given me... I mean, I was only 18-years old. I started out running the maintenance staff... then I ran the front desk staff... and before I knew it, I was sitting in boardroom meetings with Mr. Icon."

I then asked, "So here you are now, 49-years old. Do you ever think about what would have happened to you and your family if you never met The Icon?"

"Of course. Everyday. Everyday, I thank God for putting him in my life... in my family's life. When each of my siblings graduated from high school, Mr. Icon sent each of them to private universities, paying for their entire education. Today, my brothers are both attorneys... 46 and 41-years old, and both of them work for Mr. Icon as his in-house legal counsel... and my sister at 39-years old today, is a CPA by trade, and is now Mr. Icon's CFO for his men's clothing company," Francisco proudly told me.

Jokingly, I said, "Wow, it seems like your brothers and your sister got an even better deal than you!"

I knew, at that very moment, that I had stuck my foot in my mouth... again. Ironically, Francisco thought my comment was funny, as he started laughing.

He said, "Not exactly. For my 40th birthday, Mr. Icon gave me a gift that I could have never fathomed."

"What'd he give you, a Ferrari?" I joked.

"No. He gave me 10% ownership of this hotel, *The Hotel 100*. The hotel is worth approximately $225 million, so my shares alone are worth $22.5 million," Francisco said.

"Oh my God! Are you serious?" I exclaimed.

"Mr. Icon has always been overly generous with me and my family, but I never expected anything like this. He told me that he wanted to say thank you for being so loyal to him from the very beginning. He told me how much he appreciated the work I did for him back in Nicaragua at *El Cien*, helping him get his first hotel off the ground. Mr. Vincent, those were *The Good Ole Days*. Now, I know deep in my heart that he never needed me, obviously. But that's how Mr. Icon is. He always over-rewards his people, especially when they've been loyal to him," Francisco explained.

I was shocked. But then I became confused. If Francisco was worth over $22 million, why was he still working so many hours at the hotel?

But when I asked him, I felt about two feet tall.

Francisco explained, "The reason I still work so hard is to thank Mr. Icon for everything he's done for me and my family. Sure, I don't need to work this hard anymore, and quite frankly, Mr. Icon has tried to get me to take some time off, but I won't. This is my way of honoring him. Obviously, I want *The Hotel 100* to be the best because I do own 10% of it... and obviously, this is my baby, having been part of Mr. Icon's team in building it from the ground up, twenty-three years ago... but it's also part of Mr. Icon's legacy, and it's my duty – my honor – to perpetuate his legacy. He asked me to personally teach you the ropes, and it is my honor, Mr. Vincent, to teach you as Mr. Icon has taught me."

I was speechless.

Francisco's story humbled me to the core.

He had experienced so much pain and struggle in his life, that it made my so-called struggles seem petty and insignificant.

That's the thing about us Americans.

We're spoiled.

When I looked at my own life, I've never had to worry about having clean water to drink. I've never had the responsibility of raising three siblings at the tender age of fifteen.

And here was Francisco, a man that came from nothing, with the deck so heavily stacked against him that most people would have bet against him.

But not The Icon.

Instead, The Icon bet *on* him... heavily.

This seemed to be a recurring theme in The Icon's business relationships. He put great trust in people, which made me wonder if he'd ever been burned by people that he opened himself up to.

One day I would ask him that question, but not any time soon. I didn't want to put any doubts in his head about me, so I figured I should keep my mouth shut for the time being.

At the end of my shift, I thanked Francisco for being so open with me. It meant the world to me that he would be so transparent with me, especially having just met me.

But I should have known better.

So far, Andrei, Joseph and Francisco were all very open with me. They all shared their personal stories with me – even things that were extremely personal – things that most people wouldn't feel comfortable sharing openly with someone they'd just met.

But that was one of the common threads that ran through each of them... part of The Icon's influence on them, no doubt. None of these gentlemen had any insecurities about their troubled pasts.

And that's when it dawned on me.

Transparency and honesty were the qualities that The Icon respected most. Everything associated with The Icon's philosophies revolved around integrity.

Everything revolved around the truth.

As I prepared to retire for the evening, I looked forward to my second day with Joseph at the firm, and ironically, I was equally as fired up about what I would learn from Francisco on my second night working at *The Hotel 100*.

For the first time in my life, things were looking up... and I was grateful.

Chapter Seven
The Isabella Effect

Six months had gone by – the best six months of my entire life. Between my internship with Joseph, and my part-time job at *The Hotel 100* with Francisco, I felt like I had learned more in these six months than I had in my eight years of college.

All I wanted to do was work and learn.

Every day was an opportunity for me to learn – to better myself – and I took every opportunity I had to grow as a businessman and as a person.

I met with The Icon at least once a week, sometimes at *Madre's Coffee House*... sometimes in The Presidential Suite at *The Hotel 100*... and sometimes in one of the conference rooms at the firm.

I had never been so optimistic about my future.

One Saturday afternoon, right after I'd gotten off my shift at *The Hotel 100*, I got a disturbing phone call from my father as I was driving back to my apartment.

My father was a blue-collar type of guy, and he had worked hard his entire life in the construction business. He grew up in Hays, Kansas, a small town with a population of about 20,000 people, and that's where he raised our family.

He was a prideful man, and though he never came out and said it, deep down, he would have preferred that I had stayed in Hays and joined him in the construction business. My parents were never rich, but they did okay for being in a small town.

My brother Derek was seven years older than me. Derek was a star baseball player, and even at 12-years old, he already had professional scouts watching him. During his junior year in high school, just before he turned 17-years old, every major university was after him – UCLA, Stanford, Texas A&M, Wichita State – you name it.

On top of that, pro teams were drooling over him too. Everyone expected him to be a first or second round draft pick when he graduated, which would have been a huge accomplishment for a high school player.

But during the summer after his junior year, he got into a fight with the wrong guys, and after several major confrontations, the rivalry escalated to the point of no return.

One night, Derek was driving home from a party and his rivals spotted him. They trailed him for several blocks, and as they pulled their car up beside his, they unloaded two shotgun blasts, car-to-car, assault style.

Derek was shot in the back of his head by the shotgun blasts, and died right there in his car.

My brother was my idol. I always wanted to be like him, but I wasn't born with the athletic ability that he was, and no matter how much my father pushed me to be like Derek, I never quite measured up in his eyes.

When Derek died, part of my father died with him.

I was only 10-years old when he died, and for a 10-year old, shouldering the burden of being my father's last hope of having the perfect son was more pressure than I could take.

I ended up quitting baseball, and all sports for that matter, and nothing angered my father more. He resented me for that, and to this day, I could tell that he still resented me.

When I graduated from high school, I moved to Hawaii to go to college, and that's when I learned how to surf. Surfing was the best thing for me, because it allowed me to enjoy something without being judged.

It was liberating, unlike baseball.

With surfing, no one ever compared me to Derek.

My father, however, continued to compare me to my brother, which was such an unfair comparison. Derek was born an athlete, and I was not. And to make things worse, during my entire adolescent years, and even young adulthood years, everyone compared me to what they thought Derek would have eventually become.

It was an impossible thing to live up to.

When I got divorced, that was just another one of my many failures in my father's eyes. My ex-wife's decision to leave me was the ultimate level of disapproval, and it reinforced my father's lack of approval.

I had become used to not living up to other people's expectations of me. It was something that hung over my head like a dark cloud.

Perhaps that's one of the main reasons I was so overwhelmed by The Icon's generosity and interest he took in me. He was the father figure I never had.

When I answered the phone and heard my father's voice, I was excited to tell him about the last six months, everything I was learning, and the potential opportunities on the horizon. But instead of encouragement, my father had nothing but skepticism and criticism for me.

"Vincent, how much is he paying you?" my father asked.

I responded, "Uhhh, well... I'm making $10 an hour at the hotel, and my internship is an unpaid internship... so..."

"What? You're working for free? What are you, stupid? You're gonna let this rich guy use you for free labor? Can't you see that he's taking advantage of you?" my father yelled.

He continued, "And working for $10 an hour, serving people water at a hotel? If you came back to Kansas, I could get you a job making $25 an hour in construction. What the hell is wrong with you?"

My father had a way of making me feel stupid and powerless. Nothing I did was ever good enough for him, and at a time that I could have really used some positive encouragement and support from him, he destroyed me.

"But Dad, I'm really learning a lot, and you should see the guys I'm working with. This one guy, Joseph... he started out with nothing and now he's..."

"Vincent! There's no way this guy is gonna make you into a millionaire! And why would any of these guys invest any time in you. You don't have a business background. You've got no experience!" my dad shouted at me.

"Dad, if you could just meet these guys…"

"Vincent! These guys are taking you for a ride."

"But…"

"Vincent! You listen to me, son. Your wife left you. I'm not saying it's ALL your fault, but she left you. And she left because she was tired of hearing about all of your pie-in-the-sky fantasies about becoming some big shot business mogul. Haven't you learned anything from this?"

It was if my father knew exactly what to say to cut to the deepest levels of my insecurities. He was always the first one to point out my shortcomings, and as much as I wished his words didn't affect me so negatively, they did.

This wasn't the first time I'd been barraged by my father, receiving a verbal beating from his disapproval.

I was used to it.

After I hung up the phone, I was so beaten up by the discouraging conversation with my father, I couldn't even recall the last ten minutes of driving.

I felt like an inflatable raft with a leak in it, slowly deflating – little by little – to the point of barely staying afloat, and weak enough to be pulled underwater by the slightest downward tug.

I immediately called The Icon.

He picked up on the first ring.

"Vincent, my man! What's going on?" The Icon asked.

"I just got off the phone with my dad."

"Cool! Did you tell him about everything you're doing?"

I didn't know how to respond to The Icon's question. I surely didn't want to sound unappreciative of the gracious opportunity he'd granted me with, however I didn't want to lie to him either.

"Sir, let's just say that my dad isn't exactly a fan of me pursuing this entrepreneurial path."

The Icon let out a big chuckle and said, "I get it. Most parents aren't too fired up about their kids taking this path either. Basically, they don't want to see their kids suffer, but what they don't realize is that it's the suffering that makes them strong. It's the suffering that builds character."

"Sir, you and I both know that, but my dad... he just doesn't get it," I said in a solemn tone of voice.

"Hmmm... that's too bad."

"Sir, he told me to quit, and that I should move back to Kansas and work with him in the construction business," I confessed.

"Well, is that YOU want to do?"

"No! Never! No way! It's just that my dad... you know... he just says these things that make me feel... stupid, you know? He just... I mean everything I do... it's just... it's just never good enough for him."

I think The Icon could hear the pain and frustration in my voice. He listened with empathy and without judgment.

I felt stupid calling him on a Saturday afternoon, but he seemed to understand.

He said, "Listen Vincent, my wife and I were going to grill some chicken and hang out by the pool this evening. Why don't you come over to the house and have a casual dinner with us? My wife has been on my case about wanting to meet you."

"Oh, no. I don't want to impose. I shouldn't have called you on a Saturday. I'm so sorry," I apologized.

"Vincent, don't be ridiculous. My wife is... wait... hold on a second," The Icon said, sounding distracted.

Then the unexpected happened.

"Hola, Vincent! This is Isabella. My husband has been talking about you non-stop for the last six months, and I've been dying to meet you. Please come over and join us at our home this evening. It'll be fun, I promise," Mrs. Icon said in her charming South American accent.

Her voice sounded like an angel, perhaps the most charming voice I had ever heard, next to Valentina's of course.

Yes, I was still caught up with the girl at the coffee shop I'd met six months ago.

Mrs. Icon sounded so genuine on the phone, completely disarming my feelings of insecurity.

"Ma'am, I'd be honored to join you," I said.

The Icon got back on the phone with me and said, "Vincent, I'm going to text you the address right now. When you get to the guard gate, just tell them your name. I'll let them know to expect you."

This was the first time I'd ever been invited to The Icon's home. I rushed back to my apartment to freshen up, and on my way to the freeway, I stopped at a specialty liquor store to buy a nice bottle of tequila, The Icon's favorite.

I walked into the store and immediately asked for help, because I knew absolutely nothing about tequila.

An older gentleman, the store manager, came up to me and said, "So, I hear you're looking for a nice bottle of tequila."

"Yes, sir. What would you recommend?" I asked.

He walked me over to the tequila section, and said, "Is this for a gift?"

"Yes, for a very special person that is very knowledgeable about tequila... which I am not," I transparently explained.

"Okay. Do you know if he likes to sip it like brandy, or does he mix it in a margarita?" the manager asked.

"He's definitely a sipping tequila kind of guy. I think he likes the *annyaho* kind," I ignorantly stated.

The man started laughing.

"I think you mean *añejo,* which is the finest type of tequila. Would you like me to walk you through the different types?" he respectfully asked.

"That would be great," I said, gladly accepting his tequila tutorial. I figured it would be good to know what I was giving The Icon.

The manager began by explaining, "There are three main classes of tequila. You have *blanco,* or *silver* as some call it. It's clear in color. Then you have *reposado* which has a light brown tone. The reason for the tone is that it's been slightly aged in an oak barrel, giving it a mild woodsy flavor, as well as its hue. *Blanco* and *reposado* are typically used in margaritas and tequila-based mixed drinks, however if the quality of the tequila is top notch, you can sip both of them."

"Interesting," I said. "So what about the *añejo?*" I inquired.

"Okay, so the *añejo* has the darkest tone of the three, and the reason is that it's been aged the longest in the oak barrel. *Añejo* is typically the smoothest and is aromatically the most interesting, with varying complex undertones," the manager explained.

He continued, "The more you learn about fine tequila, the more you'll grow to appreciate it. For example, an agave plant takes about ten years for it to grow to the point to where it can be harvested into tequila. One plant only makes about three good bottles of tequila. Take this one for example. *Extra añejo – Reserva de Familia* – one of the finest bottles of *añejo* we carry. It retails for $385."

"$385 for a bottle of tequila?" I asked in bewilderment.

The manager chuckled and replied, "The good stuff ain't cheap. But in my opinion, the $385 bottle isn't as good as this one right here."

He pulled out an unassuming bottle, labeled *Frida Kahlo – Añejo Produccion Limitada.*

"You said this is for a gift, right?" the manager confirmed.

"Yes, for someone very special. He's kind of a tequila aficionado," I said, knowing darn well that The Icon isn't *kind of* anything. If The Icon is passionate about something, he knows that topic inside and out.

The manager replied, "Son, if he's a tequila aficionado, he'll love this one. Not too many people know about it. Most people go for the more commercialized brands, like *Patron* or *Don Julio*... but nothing, and I mean NOTHING compares to *Frida Kahlo*. This is a brand that very few people know about, and at $130 a bottle, it's a steal."

It's funny how everything, especially price, is relative. I've never spent $130 on any type of liquor. I had planned on spending about $40 - $50, which was even a stretch on my $10 an hour budget, but I wanted to show my appreciation towards The Icon and his wife, so I sucked it up and went with the $130 *Frida Kahlo*.

I also stopped by a local florist so I could give Mrs. Icon a nice bouquet of flowers. I guess my Midwest upbringing wouldn't allow me to show up empty handed.

When I got to the guardhouse in front of the entrance gate to The Icon's community, it looked like I was about to enter *The Pentagon*. They were so thorough, I'm surprised they didn't strip search me. This was some serious security.

As I drove through The Icon's neighborhood searching for his house, I was floored. I'd never seen homes like these before. Each home looked like a *mini-Ritz Carlton* resort.

These homes were between 10,000 and 20,000 square feet, and the lots looked like you could get lost on them, they were so enormous. Some of the front lawns were so humongous, you could play two football games on them at the same time.

And there it was.

The Icon's house.

It was a Spanish-style home, but to merely call it a *home* was an understatement. It was rustic in its architectural design, yet the lines were clean and modern. It had the perfect balance between antiquity and modernity.

I've always been a design buff, and ironically, or maybe not so ironically, The Icon's house looked like my dream home.

This was definitely *my style.*

I proceeded to drive through the second gate at the entrance to The Icon's property. You know you're in the big leagues when you have to drive through two gates to get to your home.

The Icon's home was ultra-private. A tall, white stucco wall surrounded the property. Giant bougainvillea vines grew on the inside of the property's walls, as beautiful giant clusters of magenta flowers cascaded down the exterior of the never-ending white stucco wall.

It reminded me of some of the massive estates I'd seen in magazines located in Montecito. I didn't realize estates of this magnitude existed in Bel Air.

As I knocked on the door, I was excited, yet terrified at the same time. I wanted so badly to make a good impression with Mrs. Icon, that as I held the bouquet of flowers in my hand, I was practically squeezing them to death.

My knuckles were white as could be, and I began to develop an uncomfortable dryness in my mouth. Just as I was about to swallow, Mrs. Icon answered the door.

"You must be Vincent! Como estas? It's a pleasure to meet you!" she enthusiastically exclaimed, giving me a big warm hug.

Mrs. Icon was 56-years old, but she didn't look a day over forty. She was devastatingly gorgeous... as in *drop-dead-devastatingly gorgeous.*

She had long dark hair – the color of Columbian Espresso – and beautiful olive skin that was so flawless, it looked like it had been *Photoshopped.* Her dark brown eyes were captivating in a way that made it difficult not to get lost, staring into them. She wore a *Versace* summer dress, and her mere presence made me feel like I was amidst royalty.

As we entered the massive foyer, I attempted to make small talk with Mrs. Icon, handing her the modest bouquet of flowers, saying, "Ma'am, these are for you."

"Oh Vincent! Qué bonito! That is so sweet of you! My husband was right. You ARE quite the gentleman! But none of this ma'am stuff, okay? Please call me Isabella. It makes me feel younger!" she exclaimed, letting out an infectious laugh.

"My husband is out back, grilling some chicken, but let me put these flowers in a vase first. They'll make a great centerpiece for our dinner! Come with me to the kitchen."

As Isabella arranged the flowers on one of her two center islands, I took an inventory of the kitchen. This was no ordinary kitchen. It looked like a cross between the set of a celebrity chef's TV cooking show and a massive art gallery.

On the walls hung huge black and white photographs, several of them spanning over six to ten feet in length.

"Something tells me there's a story behind these photographs," I said, attempting to make myself sound inquisitive.

"They're amazing, aren't they? My husband took these back when he was in Nicaragua... before he opened *El Cien*."

She walked me over to each one, enthusiastically explaining the significance of every little detail.

"I didn't realize he was into photography."

"Oh, my husband is an AMAZING photographer. He has a great eye for detail... for the aesthetic. Look at this one. This is the plot of land that he built *El Cien* on, back when it was just dirt, sand and jungle."

This was the largest of all the photographs.

A long stretch of beach, nestled in a private cove, with nothing but ocean to one side of the sand, and jungle to the other side. To think that The Icon could have visualized his *El Cien* from this blank slice of paradise explained why the photograph was so magical.

He was a man of vision, and could artistically articulate the potential of this property in a mere black and white photograph.

"So how did you and your husband meet?" I inquired.

Isabella was so enthusiastic about telling me her story. Every word that left her lips was filled with passion and life. While most people spoke in *black-and-white*, Isabella spoke in *full color*.

Isabella was born into one of the most powerful families in Barranquilla, Columbia. Her father was a business mogul in the cocoa business, but his company was funded through questionable means, and his association with a major drug cartel arose suspicions about the legitimacy of his business dealings.

What made Isabella so fascinating was that she had no reservations in telling me about her family's tarnished image or her troubled background. She, along with everyone in The Icon's inner circle, was completely transparent.

She explained, "When I was young, I fell in love with a boy – a classmate that attended the same private high school I attended – but he wasn't from a prominent family, and my father greatly disapproved of the relationship. When I turned 18, we attempted to get married in secret. But when my father discovered my covert plans, my boyfriend mysteriously disappeared. Everyone speculated that it was linked back to my father's association with the cartel. My boyfriend's body was never found."

"Oh my God," I said, mostly because I didn't know what else to say.

I could tell by Isabella's frankness that growing up in that part of Columbia – around those types of associations – that she was no stranger to that sort of thing.

"Vincent, I left Columbia with no money, and no desire to associate with my family's criminal activity. I wanted to make it on my own. I landed in New York when I was only 19-years old.

Can you believe that? 19-years old! I was just a baby! But I was determined to make it on my own. I didn't want to be in debt to anyone, and I didn't want any strings attached to my family. I was determined to be *free*."

Isabella carried herself with the self-confidence of a woman that knew who she was, and wasn't ashamed to talk about where she'd come from.

"Vincent, I took a job in a small local coffee shop, making minimum wage. I worked that job for about two years, barely scraping by to pay my bills. Sometimes I look back at those days and wonder how I even made ends meet."

It was difficult for me to picture this beautifully statuesque woman without the glamorous and luxurious lifestyle she enjoyed today.

"Vincent, I got lucky, really. One day, I was working my shift, and an agent from one of the largest modeling agencies in New York ordered coffee from me. She asked me if I ever considered becoming a model... and I laughed out loud. I never thought about anything like this before," Isabella modestly explained.

To hear Isabella say that she never viewed herself as model material seemed entirely ludicrous to me, however I could tell that she was sincere in her obliviousness to her own beauty.

"I became one of the most sought after runway models in the fashion industry. Can you believe that? Es loco, no? I've lived in Paris, Milan and New York City, and after eight years traveling the world, I met my husband here in Los Angeles. He was 33-years old back then, and I was twenty-seven. Ever since then, we've been inseparable," Isabella explained with great vigor.

Isabella had a sense of relaxed confidence that seemed to flow naturally, completely unforced and unpretentious. She had a genuinely happy spirit – one that made everything around her flow easily and effortlessly. Isabella had a magically magnetic aura that made you just want to be around her.

"My husband is an amazing man, Vincent."

I smiled, nodding my head in confirmation. "He's already changed my life, and just being here in your beautiful home with you – getting to meet you – no one's ever extended themselves to me the way your husband has."

"You know, when I first met my husband, the thing that impressed me the most about him was how open he was with people. It's one of the most valuable things I've learned from him," Isabella said with an enthusiastic yet sentimental smile.

"So how exactly did you two meet?" I inquired.

"I was modeling at a fundraising event – a charity fashion show for a non-profit organization that funds orphanages in South America. My husband was the keynote speaker that evening, and as I watched him speak, he was so dynamic – so passionate – so open with his emotions. As he poured his heart out from stage, he encouraged the other attendees to donate more towards the cause. He was so handsome in his tuxedo… so *debonair*."

Isabella told stories better than anyone I'd ever met. They were filled with such vivid detail, projecting her fabulous experiences in 3-D.

"Vincent, there were photographers following him everywhere like paparazzi. And in the midst of all the commotion, he spotted me and immediately walked directly towards me, locking eye contact with me the entire way. The photographers followed him, like he was a movie star or something, and as he approached me head on, he smiled and said, *'I heard you wanted to take your picture with me!'* Then he placed his hand on my lower back, gently pulling me closer to him, and the photographers' flashes starting exploding like a fireworks show on the 4th of July!"

"Did you actually tell someone that you wanted to get a picture with him?"

"No! Of course not!" she said, bursting into laughter.

"That's just my husband's way! He loves catching people off guard, and he has a great sense of humor. I thought to myself, *'Who does this guy think he is, telling me that he heard I wanted a picture with him?'* I was half offended and half intrigued. Any man with that kind of confidence is kind of sexy!" she said with a mischievous grin, blushing in a nostalgic sort of way.

I could just see The Icon approaching Isabella in that way, gliding across the room with his proverbial soundtrack playing in the background.

Isabella continued, "He asked me out for coffee after the event. Actually, no. He didn't ASK me out. He TOLD me that we were going to go out for coffee after the event."

Out came Isabella's mischievous grin again.

"You know Vincent, back then, most men would try to woo me with their money, or their cars, trying to wine and dine me. But not my husband. He took me out for coffee! That's it! We went to this small, obscure little Cuban coffee shop called *Café Cubano* and we had…"

"Let me guess. Grande Americanos… three Splendas… and a dash of cream."

"Yes!" she exclaimed, bursting into laughter again, warming the room like rays of sunshine.

"But I ordered mine with an extra shot of Espresso," she said coyly, grinning with that *Isabella grin* again.

I think she knew about the *Extra Shot Of Espresso Club* that The Icon and Andrei had created, and silently reveled in the fact that she was the original source of their *members-only* coffee concoction.

After she finished arranging my flowers, she said, "Come Vincent. Let me show you around."

Isabella gave me a quick tour of their home.

Well, I guess it wasn't *that* quick, being that it's impossible to *quickly* tour a 20,000 square-foot home that sat on several acres of land.

The floors were made of *koa* wood, a very expensive wood, indigenous to Hawaii. I remember being in college in Hawaii, and hearing about how expensive *koa* wood was. I hadn't ever seen it used in homes outside of Hawaii due to the cost, but for The Icon, *cost* was never an issue.

The walls were all done in Venetian plaster.

Isabella explained that they had flown in the top Venetian plaster artisan from Florence, Italy to have him do the entire house. The detail in his work was nothing short of masterful. Its smooth texture and marbleized finish captured a million-and-one different earth tones.

The vaulted ceilings had exposed, distressed beams throughout the home, but they weren't just any old beams.

The beams were *reclaimed* beams that came from an old church in Oaxaca, Mexico and were over 200 years old. The Icon had purchased these rare gems through an art dealer in Santa Barbara. They were magnificent – each beam, one of a kind.

The design of the home and the décor was impeccable, yet also very warm and inviting, and as huge and impressive as it was, it didn't feel like I was walking through a museum. It felt like a *home* – a home filled with many fantastic stories and memories – a home rich in family love.

As we walked through this incredible estate, we headed into the backyard, which looked like a luxury resort, Isabella proudly carrying with her my floral arrangement.

We walked down a long walkway that was lined with beautiful white rose bushes, as massive bougainvillea vines grew up onto a trellis that covered the 200-foot walkway. It looked like the kind of walkway that a royal family's wedding procession would march down.

The pool was equally as impressive as its water level was flush with the pool deck, which was entirely made of travertine. This massive body of water looked like a mirage, and was so big, it looked like it could have floated *The Titanic* in it.

And there was The Icon, under a giant palapa-covered pavilion at the head of the pool, manning the grill. The pavilion was big enough to host a 100-person wedding event, with a full bar, huge white sectional sofas that looked too expensive to keep outdoors, and giant ceiling fans that looked like giant helicopter propellers.

As I entered the resort-within-the-resort, salsa music played through the state-of-the-art surround sound system whose speakers were invisible, hidden in the rafters.

"Vincent! My man!" The Icon exclaimed. "You've obviously met my wife, Isabella. She's been dying to meet you!"

Every interaction I had with The Icon was empowering. He had a magical way of making everyone feel special and welcome. He was always so enthusiastic. But what made his enthusiasm so special was that he always seemed to be more enthusiastic about the other person than whatever he had going on in his life, and believe me, he always had A LOT going on in his life.

The Icon made everyone around him feel like *the star*, which actually made him shine brighter. He was never afraid of letting other people shine – one of the qualities I would learn to respect most about him.

"Sir, thank you so much for inviting me into your home," I said, handing him the bottle of tequila like I was presenting him with a *Grammy Award*.

"Babe! Look at this! Vincent brought a bottle of *Frida* with him!" The Icon exuberantly told his wife. He looked at me with enthusiasm and said, "Vincent, how'd you know about *Frida*? This is my favorite tequila!"

It made me feel good to be able to give The Icon something that he enjoyed so much. Plus the fact that it made me look like I was *in-the-know* didn't hurt either.

When it came to selecting a gift for a man with as specific a taste as The Icon, I knew that a great deal of thought was required.

But not because he was an elitist, and certainly not because he expected it.

The Icon was a gracious and appreciative soul. But because he was the kind of man that would put in as much thought

– if not more thought – into hand selecting a gift for you, you wanted to your gift to be equally as special.

"Papi, you were right. Vincent is quite the gentleman! Look at this lovely bouquet of flowers he brought us," she said, smiling at her husband.

It was obvious that Isabella was used to very elaborate – very expensive – floral arrangements. There were so many fresh floral arrangements throughout the house, it looked as if they were planning to host a lavish wedding reception in the foyer alone.

Nevertheless, she still made a big production of my very modest gift, making me feel special.

Both she and The Icon had that ability.

Isabella had the sweetest way about her, yet her keen sense of humor made her spicy too. She was witty and sharp.

You could tell she knew how to win people over, not in a manipulative way, but in a gracious way.

She, along with The Icon, had mastered the ability to make people feel good about themselves.

Watching the two of them interact with each other made me understand why they'd been happily married for thirty-two years. They were perfect for each other.

As we sat down for dinner, The Icon brought up my disturbing conversation with my father. I told him the whole story as both he and Isabella listened intently.

"I just don't understand why my dad has to say things like that. No matter what I do, it's never good enough for him. I don't think he's ever been proud of anything I've ever done in my life."

It was as if they both completely understood what I was going through.

I continued, "Why doesn't he... I just don't know why he can't..." I paused, staring at the floor – shifting the weight from my toes back into my heels – unable to find my words. My voice began to mumble as my heart sank deeper into my chest cavity. I fought to hold back my tears. I didn't want to make The Icon or Isabella feel uncomfortable.

It physically hurt my heart every time I thought about disappointing my father. I had racked up so many disappointments and disapprovals with him, I would have thought I'd have grown callous to it by now.

But I never did.

With each disappointment, the cumulative scoreboard of disappointments continued to grow. I was *disappointing*, and an overall *disappointment*, embodying both the adjective and the noun derivative of the word.

There were times that I cursed him out in the privacy of my innermost thoughts, casting aside his disapproval, invalidating his opinions of me and my life's outcome. This was the fantasy world I would retreat into – the fantasy world of expressing my true feelings – being able to speak my mind without reservation, fear or insecurity.

But this world – the world I had created in my mind – was just fantasyland.

Deep down, I wished I had the guts to stand up for myself.

I wished I could be strong enough in my own resolve to let the negative comments and opinions about me bounce right off of me like a beach ball.

And I wished I didn't care so much about what my father thought of me.

However, these wishes were just that.

Wishes.

I could never seem to escape the guilt of not living up to my father's standards, and I always sought out his approval.

But I always fell short.

As I disclosed my vulnerabilities and embarrassing insecurities to these two gracious hosts, The Icon and Isabella studied me with eyes of empathy and compassion. It was as if they took my experience personally, internalizing my pain.

I felt validated and guilty at the same time.

Here I was, dumping my pain onto two people that I was just getting to know, and they treated me the way that an ideal set of parents would unconditionally treat their own blood.

Then The Icon said to me, "Vincent, let me share something with you that I don't share with most people."

He pulled up his chair to the table, just three-quarters of an inch closer, as if to imply that I would somehow be able to hear his words more clearly by decreasing the physical distance between us.

He glanced briefly at Isabella, as she smiled and nodded her head, as if to endorse the idea of The Icon sharing something very personal with me. It was as if she knew what he was going to share with me. That's how connected the two of them were to each other.

"Vincent, I never got along with my father either. He never supported my dreams of becoming a successful entrepreneur. He wanted me to follow in his footsteps and become an attorney. My father was a very successful defense attorney... one of the best in the world. But I saw him represent criminals. He was such a talented attorney that he won huge cases, even when he knew his clients were guilty. Mob clients. Major criminals. That never sat right with me."

"But with all of your success, he must be proud of you now, right?" I assumingly asked.

"Actually, my father passed away before I became successful. I had worked on trying to find the right business during my 20's, and I'd racked up several failures. He saw me struggle year after year, and he didn't understand why I didn't just go to law school and take over his firm. He was furious with me because I didn't want to follow in his footsteps. He never believed I'd ever become successful as a gun-slinging entrepreneur," The Icon explained.

I could tell that there was a part of him that was still hurt by the lack of support he received from his father. I think every man, regardless of his age, seeks the approval of his father to a certain degree. I was certainly in this category myself, and ironically, it appeared that The Icon fell into this category as well.

The Icon continued, "My father died when I was in Nicaragua building my first hotel, *El Cien*. I would talk to him over the phone occasionally, and every time I told him how well things were going, he'd always put me down, telling me that I should have been an attorney. He never saw *El Cien*. I really wish he could have seen it. It was really something."

I didn't understand how any father wouldn't be proud of someone as accomplished as The Icon. As I listened intently to The Icon recounting his incomplete relationship with this father, I watched Isabella running her fingers through his hair. They were so connected with one another, that even in her silence, she consoled The Icon's pain.

He continued to tell me about his father, and the more he divulged, the more connected I became with The Icon. He suffered from the same issues I suffered from in this area. Perhaps that's what created the special bond between us.

"Vincent," he said, "I spent many years of my life being bitter at my father, wanting him to accept me and my business pursuits. I used to really begrudge him, saying that I needed his support back then. But I guess I really didn't *need* his support, because I became successful without it."

That's when I learned *Rule Number Ten: Never blame others*.

"Vincent, finger-pointers are failures. You must take responsibility for your actions and your results. The reason people attempt to blame others, pointing their finger at someone else, is that they feel there's something wrong with failing at something. But as an entrepreneur, you've got to understand that there's nothing wrong with crashing and burning. In fact, the more you're willing to crash and burn, the more of a chance you have at becoming massively successful. There's no shame in having projects that fail, and blaming others certainly doesn't increase your chances of your next project succeeding either. A winner takes his failures like a man and gets back up. A winner understands that these so-called failures are often times essential to his glorious success because of the valuable lessons learned in the process. Embrace them, because they're essential. Don't waste your time blaming yourself or blaming others," said The Icon.

The Icon's words made me think more about my father's lack of support and discouraging words. As much as I wanted him to be more supportive, I realized that I was using him as a crutch.

I was playing the martyr role, blaming my father for my lack of success. Sure, in a perfect world, he'd be the one cheering me on, but life isn't perfect. I was using my father's lack of support as an excuse to not succeed.

Without telling me this bluntly, The Icon was making his point, and I got it.

"You see Vincent, the only one that can stand in your way, is you. Everyone else is just a spectator, nothing more. If your dad doesn't encourage you, that's a real shame... for him. I know it hurts because it still hurts me too. But I also know that my number one responsibility is to my wife," The Icon said.

Isabella put her arms around The Icon and said, "It's me and you against the world," squeezing him close to her chest.

"That's right, baby," The Icon said, smiling. "Show Vincent your watch."

Isabella took off her rose gold *Rolex* and showed me the inscription that read *Us Against The World* and explained, "You see Vincent, at the end of the day, the only thing that matters is the life you build for you and your nuclear family, and it starts with the relationship you build with your wife. It's going to be you and her against the world. Look at my father. He had money. He had power. But he was a criminal. I wanted nothing to do with that life. When I met my husband, I was nervous about telling him of my past, because I was ashamed of it. But he helped me realize that it's not where you're from that's important. It's where you're going in life that matters."

Listening to Isabella was like listening to a prophet. She was so well spoken, as she had a level of wisdom and a quality about her soul that was incredibly comforting.

"My husband has taught me a lot about life, including the importance of letting go of the past," Isabella said.

And just as she said that, The Icon quickly jumped in saying, "Vincent, if you want to know the real truth, it's Isabella that has taught ME about life... like how to laugh... how to love... how to enjoy the moment. I owe my life to her."

To hear The Icon say that he owed his life to Isabella was perhaps the most powerful thing I'd ever heard. Everyone whose life The Icon had touched seemed to feel as though they owed him everything, including Isabella. But for The Icon, it was apparent that Isabella had added a dimension to his life that only Isabella could have.

Watching them interact inspired me to find *my* Isabella. This was the kind relationship I wanted. This was the kind marriage I wanted.

Us Against The World.

I loved that kind of commitment... that kind of undying loyalty... that kind of bond.

As we finished dinner, The Icon pulled me aside and said, "Vincent, meet me at *Madre's* tomorrow morning for coffee. There's something I want to talk to you about, man to man."

As the evening came to an end, I was once again reminded how fortunate I was.

Sure, my dad was being his normal, disempowering self.

Sure I was only making ten bucks an hour.

Sure I was working 16-hour days.

But I was excited about who I was becoming.

I distinctly remember saying that to myself several times. I was excited about who I was becoming in the process of this whirlwind... and I was grateful.

Chapter Eight
Us Against The World

The following morning, I met The Icon for coffee at *Madre's*. This time I actually beat him there.

I ordered two Grande Americanos with three Splendas and a dash of cream for the two of us. His had an extra shot of Espresso in it, while I was still trying to earn my right of passage. I was careful to not overstep my boundaries.

As The Icon floated in the front door, he saw me sitting at a table with the two Americanos, and smiled. He was always aware of the details.

A man of The Icon's status wasn't used to having people pick up the tab for things. Sure, it was just coffee, but I wanted him to know that I appreciated him, and that I wasn't the type of person that expected him to always pay, just because he was the one with all the money.

I hated these people that always assumed that the *rich guy* should pick up the bill. It was the welfare mentality, and I did my very best to make it known to The Icon that I didn't subscribe to that mindset.

I wanted to constantly prove my character to him.

Above all, *character* was what The Icon respected most.

I jokingly welcomed him saying, "Sir, welcome back to *Madre's*. Your Americano... three Splendas with a dash of cream and an extra shot of Espresso... compliments of your Protégé."

I wanted him to know that I was absorbing everything that Francisco was teaching me at *The Hotel 100*, and I didn't dare tell him that I knew that Isabella originated the *members-only* Americano.

The Icon chuckled out loud saying, "Vincent! You're really mastering Francisco's teachings about effective communication I see. I'm impressed... and you have a great sense of humor. That's a great quality to have."

I always wanted to impress The Icon, letting him know I was taking every lesson I learned to heart.

"So Vincent, you're probably wondering why I wanted to meet with you this morning," The Icon said.

"Yes, sir. Is everything okay?" I asked in a worrisome voice.

The Icon let out a good chuckle that made me feel more comfortable that I hadn't done something wrong.

"A lot of times, when people first meet Isabella, they get intimidated, feeling like they might not measure up. Now as you experienced, Isabella is a master at disarming that feeling because she puts people at ease, making them feel comfortable... making them feel good about themselves," The Icon said.

He was right. Isabella was a powerhouse.

An ex-supermodel.

Intelligent.

Accomplished.

Polished.

And of course, The Icon's wife.

But her ability to empower people was no less potent than The Icon's. It was a different kind of empowerment, but equally as significant nonetheless.

I could see how some women might be intimidated by Isabella at first glance, but it only took her about three seconds to make them feel right at home.

The Icon then asked, "Vincent, after meeting Isabella, have you thought more about what you want in a woman?"

"Absolutely!" I exclaimed. "She's amazing."

The Icon shared, "You know, one of the qualities that I always wanted in a wife was *drive*. I wanted a wife that understood my drive, and I felt that the only way she was going to understand that was if she had personally done what I had done… building a career from nothing. I wanted a self-made woman."

I concurred. When I thought about my ex-wife, one of the main reasons my marriage fell apart was that I never felt like she supported me in my career. She would constantly complain about me coming home late, or working on the weekends.

She was a constant nag, and I resented her for it. She never believed in my dream, and had about as much vision as a blindfolded man with cataracts… in the dark.

I told The Icon, "I envision my wife as being someone who has walked a parallel path as I'm walking with you right now. I want someone that appreciates the sacrifices I'm willing to make. I guess what I'm saying is that I want what you have with Isabella. I want a woman that looks at me the way Isabella looks at you, and believes in the *Us Against The World* philosophy."

The Icon responded, "Ah, yes. Well, last night we talked about the concept of *Us Against The World* and I wanted to clarify what Isabella and I meant about that. A great marriage isn't about being perfect. In fact, it's just the opposite. A great marriage is about the commitment that a husband has to his wife, and that a wife has to her husband. It's about knowing that your partner has flaws, and also knowing that you have flaws, and collectively deciding to each work on those flaws, without judgment. It's about accepting the fact that we human beings will never be perfect, but committing to the process of self-improvement in every area of your life. You see, while the rest of the world judges you for your imperfections, within a great marriage, we must seek to support and encourage each other without judgment, but with a constructive eye. Isabella and I are constantly talking about what we can do to enrich our marriage… to better our communication… and to better clarify what's most important in our lives. Now, all that being said, I just want to make sure you don't want this kind of relationship just because I wanted this for myself. Remember, *Rule Number Four*."

He was subtly reminding me that I needed to formulate my own preferences, and not just emulate his decisions. Of course I was curious about his perspectives on this issue, but it was because I saw what he had with Isabella, and I wanted that. It represented everything opposite about my previous marriage to my dumb ex-wife.

"Sir, I understand. I'm not asking you for your advice on this one. It's just that I really do agree with your philosophy about needing to have a wife that has struggled through adversities and overcome them. I want a self-made woman. I want a powerful woman that can hold her own in the same way that Isabella can. You can't be a driven man and be with a chick that hasn't walked the walk," I proclaimed.

The Icon smiled.

I had been the recipient of this smile from him before. It let me know that I had overstepped my boundaries.

"Vincent, I'm glad you feel so strongly about this issue as it pertains to your own life. It's important to have a strong resolve in what you want in life, especially when it comes to finding a wife. But you must be careful to not become judgmental of other people's marriages. What's important to you may not be important to someone else," The Icon cautioned me.

"But if a man is driven, how can he be with someone that doesn't share the same vision as he does?" I asked.

"Well, you make a good point. In any great marriage, both the husband and the wife must share the same vision. No doubt about it. But what you're missing is that a couple can have the same vision, and play different roles in their relationship. Take Joseph for example. His wife Christine is a real champ, and she's never *walked the walk* under your definition," The Icon stated.

I had met Christine a small handful of times.

She was sweet, and was definitely in love with Joseph. It was obvious that she was an amazing mother to their two kids, and was Joseph's greatest cheerleader.

But I must admit, it always puzzled me how Joseph could be so driven, and be married to a woman that wasn't as driven as he was. She seemed content just being a stay-at-home mom, and didn't have much understanding of Joseph's business whatsoever.

I know this sounds judgmental to say, but she seemed kind of *average*. She was a sweetheart and everything, but I didn't understand what Joseph saw in her. Their personalities were so different.

Joseph was a Type-A driver. He was a machine, relentless in his pursuit to take over the world, and Christine didn't seem to aspire to achieve anything close to that.

To be frank, she reminded me of one of those trophy wives you see in Newport Beach, driving the Range Rover and getting manicures and pedicures every other day.

"Vincent, what do you know about Christine?" The Icon asked.

"Well, she's cute in an *ex-captain of the cheerleading squad* sort of way… and she seems nice," I admitted.

"Vincent, let me tell you something about Christine. She's more than just a cute, nice girl. She married Joseph right before he started at the firm, back when he had nothing. She believed in him before he became the Joseph you see today," The Icon explained.

"But sir, anyone with half a brain could have probably figured out that Joseph was going to be a big hitter, including Christine," I rebutted.

"Perhaps you have a point there, but there was no guarantee. It's not like Joseph signed a big contract guaranteeing he was going to make the big bucks. He started out on straight commission, just like all the other Junior Advisors at the firm. It was Christine that supported him financially for the first year of their marriage." The Icon said.

"That's only a year. That's nothing," I said.

"Vincent, let me give you a little more insight into her story. You see, Christine came from a pretty traditional family in Newport Beach. Her father had climbed the corporate ladder and was *Vice-President of Sales* with a software company, and he did pretty well for a corporate guy. He wasn't making the kind of money Joseph makes now, but he was doing okay, pulling in a couple hundred grand per year. Her mom was a stay-at-home mom, and raised Christine and her three sisters. When Joseph and Christine started dating in college, her parents didn't think much of it, but when Joseph started his career, Christine's father disapproved of the direction he was going with a commission-only career," The Icon said.

"Why? I thought Joseph did pretty well his first couple of years," I questioned.

"He did, but Christine's father was a traditional corporate guy and thought straight-commission positions were too risky. Even when Joseph was doing well during his first two years, his success was still dismissed by Christine's dad. So when his third year hit, and he barely made a dime, her dad was all over him," said The Icon.

The Icon informed me that was the year they got married, when Joseph was *broke*.

But I still wasn't impressed.

He continued, "When Joseph started with me at the firm, it took him a while before he started closing deals. In fact, he got off to one of the slowest starts of any Junior Advisor at the firm. Basically, they lived off Christine's income to pay the bills for the first two years of their marriage. Joseph wasn't bringing in much of anything for the first year. The second year, he started doing okay, but he had racked up so much credit card debt that most of his income went to pay down his credit card bills. The whole time, Christine worked a job that she hated, but she stuck it out because she believed in Joseph. That was their plan, to use Christine's job to fund the start up of Joseph's career."

"I'm still not impressed," I said.

"Vincent, her family was constantly putting down Joseph during the first couple of years of their marriage. They'd tell him that a real man supports his wife, not the other way around. But Christine stuck to her guns, and never backed down, defending Joseph. She would get in a ton of arguments with her parents because she wouldn't let them talk down to Joseph. She really had his back," The Icon said.

I inquired, "So what happened in Joseph's second year with you?"

"Joseph's work ethic was incredible. He worked harder than anyone I've ever mentored. You see, Joseph doesn't have some of the God-given talent that I was born with. It took him a little longer to grasp new concepts, and so he had to make up for it with work ethic. He wouldn't get home to be with Christine until midnight on most nights, and she never complained. In fact, she decided to take on a second job as a cocktail waitress during the evenings to bring in a little more income to pay down their credit card bills. They'd both get home around midnight from work. I know Joseph felt guilty about their situation, but Christine reassured him that the reason she was willing to do this was because she believed in him. She knew how important it was to Joseph to build this incredible life for his family, and so she decided that she would sacrifice everything to help him make this happen," The Icon explained.

Though the story about Christine didn't *change* my mind about what I wanted in my own life, hearing The Icon talk about her story began to *open* my mind.

It made me realize that there were different types of marriage relationships that work.

I think I was so jaded by my experience with my ex-wife that I felt I needed a co-pilot… someone who had walked in my shoes and understood firsthand what I was going through.

My ex-wife just didn't understand what it was like to shoot for the stars and attempt to build something out of nothing. She didn't have an ounce of entrepreneurial spirit in her.

As I think back, I really resented her for that.

She was like so many women. They want to live the life of luxury, but they don't want to pay the price.

Before I had even met The Icon, I knew that success, in most cases, didn't come easy. In addition, it usually didn't come overnight either. I was willing to grind it out and pay my dues, but my ex-wife wanted everything yesterday.

I never understood these spoiled princess-type chicks.

They want the *million dollar lifestyle,* but they expect their husbands to be home from work every night at 6:00 p.m.

They're delusional.

Successful people, especially during the building stages of their career, had to put in long hours. They had to sacrifice in the short-term in order to reap benefits in the long-term.

There was much I didn't understand back then during my naïve inexperienced years, but at least I understood that.

Success, in most cases, had to be *earned.*

Some of these women that live in la-la land even expect their husbands to pick up the phone every time they call them in the middle of a workday.

That's about as unrealistic as a professional basketball player calling a timeout because his wife's calling him on his cell phone in the middle of the fourth quarter of Game 7 in the NBA finals.

In all fairness, I realized that I was no *NBA star,* but the concept was still valid.

I just really wanted a wife that understood the game as a *player.* I didn't want to be married to a mere *spectator.*

But I also learned that just because I had my preferences about the vision I had for my own marriage, didn't mean it was ideal for everyone else.

Joseph certainly seemed to be happy in his marriage, and the bond he had with Christine was no less special than the bond that The Icon had with Isabella – different, but no less special.

I thought about the kind of woman that would go against her own parents because they disapproved of her man... the kind of woman that would make sacrifices for the home team... the kind of woman that wouldn't complain about what she didn't have, but instead would play any role necessary to help her husband win.

That was a *real* woman.

This conversation with The Icon made me realize that there was more than one *right* type of co-pilot.

For him, it was Isabella.

For Joseph it was Christine.

Two very different types of marriages and two very different types of women. However the one thing that both of these women had in common was their undying loyalty to their husbands. I got the feeling that both of them would fight tooth and nail to defend their husband's name.

That's what I wanted... a woman that would have my back, and defend my name at all costs.

I remember thinking about how few women there were out there with this kind of character. It was kind of depressing when I thought about it, because the odds were definitely not in my favor. Finding a woman like this – a true co-pilot – was like finding a needle in a field of haystacks, and I began to doubt whether or not I would ever find my *Isabella*.

But I decided that instead of focusing on what I thought was *available*, that I would focus on what I really *wanted*.

Because despite the odds not being in my favor, I understood THE most important thing when it came to the numbers game.

I only needed to find *one*.

Chapter Nine
Finding The Right Co-Pilot

The next week flew by, and as much as I enjoyed working, I also enjoyed developing my personal relationship with The Icon and with Joseph.

Joseph had invited me to have dinner with him and his wife Christine at their home.

Neither The Icon nor Joseph seemed to have any reservations about inviting me into their homes to meet their families. I found this to be odd and quite fascinating, because I'd never been invited into any of my previous bosses' homes.

This seemed to be a recurring theme with The Icon and all of his people – this theme of *trust*.

The Icon was far from naïve, and I'm sure that every time he extended himself to other people, it was a calculated risk. And I'm sure there were people that took advantage of his openness and generosity. But it didn't seem to prevent him from allowing people to get close to him. He seemed to enjoy bringing selected people into his world.

Joseph was no different in this respect.

Joseph lived in Calabasas, about a 25-minute drive from Beverly Hills. It seemed that a lot of celebrities were starting to move out to Calabasas because they could achieve two things that Beverly Hills couldn't provide: Privacy and land. The only way you could have these two things in Beverly Hills or Bel Air is if you had *Icon money*.

I looked up The Icon's house online to see what it was valued at. I know that seems rather stalkerish, but that's a sign of the times. *Everything* is available online.

His home was valued at $37 million, which even for a movie star, was a lot of money. I calculated that his property taxes alone were somewhere around $460,000 per year.

Joseph's home was valued at $8 million, but if it were located in the middle of Bel Air like The Icon's, it would have been worth three times that.

It had a similar look to The Icon's home – *Spanish Hacienda Style*. The entire property was enclosed, with massive fortress-style walls covered in *creeping fig* vines.

It was beautifully landscaped, with tons of palm trees, banana plants, and rows of giant blue agave plants.

The entrance had two huge sets of antique double doors that originally belonged to a church in Guatemala and were over 100 years old. Each set of doors were over 10-feet tall.

The first set of doors allowed you to enter the courtyard, which looked like a Spanish oasis. A giant candelabra cactus stood 20-feet tall next to a massive stone water fountain that had the perfect amount of water trickling down it to provide a soothing sound that practically put you in a trance the moment you walked in.

A giant wisteria vine crept through the massive trellis that covered the entire courtyard, and was in full-bloom. The aroma of the purple wisteria flowers that hung from the trellis was so fragrant, it made you feel like each flower was shooting little spritzes of perfume into the air, solely for your personal inhaling pleasure.

As I walked through this amazing courtyard to the front door of the house, I marveled at the architecture of Joseph's home. The exterior was done in white stucco, and had beautiful archways that practically begged you to step onto the terracotta tiled patio, sit down on one of the rustic leather rocking chairs, and write an Ernest Hemmingway inspired novel.

I knocked on the second set of antique double doors – the main entrance to the house – and moments later, Joseph answered the door.

"Vincent! Welcome! Let's step into the kitchen so you can see all the action," Joseph exclaimed.

I followed him into the most massive kitchen I'd ever seen. From the 15-foot vaulted ceiling hung a giant one-of-a-kind antique wrought iron chandelier – a generous housewarming gift from The Icon and Isabella.

Joseph's kitchen was bigger than my entire studio apartment, and in the middle of it was a giant center island made of a continuous beautiful slab of black soapstone that Joseph's kids sat at, making pizzas.

"Vincent, it's *Pizza Rustica Night*! We're all making our own gourmet pizzas tonight. I hope that's okay with you," Christine said, as she continued to chop fresh basil, heirloom tomatoes, and freshly made buffalo mozzarella cheese.

"It's our kids' favorite. Everything was grown organically in our backyard. It's kind of a ritual we do with our kids at least once a month. We'll go into our backyard, pick all the fresh vegetables, fire up our wood-burning brick pizza oven, and make our own pizzas," Joseph said.

"You have a wood-burning brick pizza oven?" I asked.

"Yeah, come check this out," Joseph said, motioning me to follow him just outside the kitchen.

There was another courtyard, one of too many courtyards to count, right outside the kitchen. It had a full outdoor kitchen with a huge stainless steel grill, four stovetop burners, a huge stainless steel refrigerator, and an authentic wood-burning brick pizza oven.

"Vincent, you're going to love this. This is the best pizza you're ever going to have. Christine makes her own pizza dough. We even have the water we use to make the pizza dough flown in from New York. There's something in the tap water in New York that makes it taste different. That's why everyone says that New York pizza is the best. It's because of the water they use to make the dough," Joseph enthusiastically shared with me.

I watched Joseph's two sons make their own pizzas. Timmy, who was eight years old, intensely concentrated on his masterpiece, cutting his pizza dough with the utmost precision.

His pizza was in the shape of a person's face, with every little detail just perfect. As I watched him, I envisioned him growing up to become some sort of master maxillofacial surgeon, perhaps even being the star of a famous makeover reality TV show one day.

Joseph's younger son James was six years old, and was the entertainer of the family. He also made his pizza in the shape of a man's face, but wasn't as intent on perfecting the shape of his pizza as he was acting out the character's persona he gave it. It was hilarious watching James's ventriloquist exhibition with his pizza dummy.

I joined in the fun with James, making my pizza's name *Burt* while his was named *Ernie*. Timmy occasionally looked up and laughed at our shenanigans, but then quickly returned to creating his work of art with the intensity of a mad scientist.

I found myself thinking about what my kids would be like someday, and what kind of father I would be.

Joseph and Christine were so connected to their sons, they seemed at ease with everything. That's probably why James and Timmy seemed so well adjusted. They had grown up in a home environment that was stable, both emotionally and financially.

They knew they were secure.

When I was growing up, it was just the opposite. I'd hear my parents constantly arguing. Many a night, I would go to bed pulling the covers over my head as I listened to my mom nagging my dad, and my dad yelling back at my mom with his verbal assault.

Their fights were usually about money, or more specifically, the lack thereof.

I probably blocked out a lot of those memories to keep my sanity as a kid, but I do remember feeling like I was always walking on eggshells.

When Derek died, it got even worse. Perhaps that's why I was a late bloomer, socially. I was always a timid kid in my adolescent years, probably from being shell shocked from my dad's constant verbal abuse.

I'm sure Joseph and Christine got into a few arguments from time to time. I mean, there's no such thing as a perfect marriage, but they had a bond that was deeper than most married couples I'd seen. They were so in sync with each other, it was like they were one entity.

As Joseph pulled each pizza out of the wood-fired brick oven, the smoky aroma was incredible. The smoke from the fire gently dissipated through a chimney, diverting it into the warm summer sky, but there was just enough that lingered in the courtyard to let you know something magical was happening in that wood-burning oven.

I did, for a moment, feel like I was in the hills of Tuscany, sipping my *Chianti Classico* wine, nibbling on some fabulous bruschetta that Christine had made with her garden's heirloom tomatoes.

"We had this thing custom built by a guy that's been building wood-fired ovens for over 30 years. The exterior is made out of this special double-walled concrete-composite material so the kids won't burn their hands if they accidently touch it. And then we had him finish it with an Old-World Tuscan *giallo* glaze," Joseph explained.

The entire experience was cool. The adults could enjoy their *adult time*, and the kids could sit right next to Joseph and Christine, entertaining themselves independently, enjoying every minute of it.

I thought to myself, "This is what you can do when you have money."

As Christine served each of us our own pizza, James and Timmy were doing their own versions of *The Happy Dance*. I could tell that this was the highlight of their month.

Christine said, "They look forward to this every month, Vincent, especially when our garden is producing heirloom tomatoes like this. When they're out of season, we just buy tomatoes at the store, but when the kids pick them from our garden, they get even more excited. It's a whole production, as you can see!"

She was right. Their kids loved the process.

"It's a time for us to enjoy time together as a family. I hope that when James and Timmy are adults, that we'll still do this together each month, kind of like a family ritual," Joseph said.

I was sure that Joseph's wish would come true. You could tell just by watching the interaction between Joseph and his kids.

He was a great father now, and I knew that as his sons matured from boys into men, that Joseph would blossom into an amazing mentor to them. He was an amazing mentor to me, and I wasn't even blood-related to him.

He was the kind of person that you just wanted to be around, both professionally and socially.

As dinner came to an end, Christine excused herself to bathe James and Timmy and put them to bed. Joseph and I reloaded our glasses of *Chianti Classico* and made our way into the living room.

"So The Icon told me about how you and Christine started off your marriage and your career at the same time," I said.

"Yeah, those were *The Good Ole Days*. Her father was a difficult man to deal with, and quite frankly, he's still a big pain in the butt," Joseph said laughing, in a good-humored way.

"So what was his beef?" I asked him.

Joseph replied, "Well, you know, he's a corporate guy. Always has been, and always will be. He's done okay in his life, but he's always been an *employee*. Not that there's anything wrong with that, but he's never been an entrepreneur, so he doesn't understand how us crazy entrepreneurs think. From his very first job up until now, he's always worked for a paycheck, trading hours for dollars, and so when he met me, he thought I was a naïve big-talker. I was always talking about running my own firm, and making more in a month than what doctors make in a year, and I guess that kind of threatened him."

"*Threatened* him? What did he have to feel threatened about?" I inquired.

"Vincent, it's going to happen to you too one day, when you're a super successful entrepreneur. You see, Christine's dad has always secretly wished that he had the GUTS to do what you and I are doing. He wishes he had the guts to go out on his own and build something from nothing... but he doesn't. He'd never be able to handle the pressure and the stress of the unknown. He needs his fancy little title, his matching 401(k) plan and his health insurance benefits. He craves security over adventure. He wants his corporate expense account so he can claim he took a client out to dinner at a nice restaurant, when in reality, he took his wife out to dinner and expensed it to his company. Corporate guys do this all the time. Essentially, they're liars and petty thieves, because they're stealing money from their boss," Joseph explained.

"So why do you say Christine's dad felt threatened by you?" I asked.

"Because I don't need a title – I own part of the firm – so you can call me anything you want. Call me the janitor, I don't care. And I don't need a corporate expense account – I can afford to pay for my own dinner. Christine and I go out to these expensive hot-shot restaurants, and as I look around, I can tell that half of these guys are trying to look like *big shots*, but they're paying for dinner with their corporate credit card and expensing it to their employer. Not only is it unethical, because they're lying about how they're using company funds, but they're lying to themselves because they're living a fabricated lifestyle that isn't even their own. That's what Christine's father had done his entire life... faking his way through, acting as if he was a guy like me. He isn't even close to being a guy like me, and he knows it. He's jealous of me because deep down, he wishes he had the guts to go for it like I did. That's why he feels so threatened," Joseph explained.

"So how was he during your first couple of years with The Icon? You were kind of struggling, right?" I inquired.

"Oh man, Christine's father was all over my case. He was betting against me the whole time! You see, I had two really big years during my rookie and sophomore year, due to my father's ability to get me in front of guys he'd done business with, but when that well dried up, I had nothing... and that's the year Christine and I got married. She was actually the one that suggested that I pursue an opportunity with The Icon. She'd heard me constantly talking about him and how successful he was, and she told me that if I wanted to be the best, that I should go learn from the best. And that's what I did," Joseph explained.

"You mean it was Christine's idea for you to pursue a career with The Icon?" I questioned.

"Vincent, if you had any idea what Christine has done for me... we truly have a partnership. I know that may sound cliché, but she really played a huge role in my success. It was her idea for me to call his office everyday for 26 days in a row. It was her idea for me to show up at his office with the $300 bottle of tequila. And it was her idea for me to put 100% of my faith in The Icon. If it wasn't for her, I might have given up," Joseph said.

I watched this incredibly successful man that I had grown to idolize for his strength and confidence, humble himself in front of me, giving his wife all the credit in the world. It became apparent that Christine was more than just a cute cheerleader. She was an instrumental part of Joseph's rise to the top.

"Vincent, you have no idea what it was like for me to have to look at Christine in the eyes, after talking about my aspirations of grandeur, knowing that she had to work two jobs to support the two of us. She hated her job, but she never once complained about our situation. She kept telling me, *'We're in this together. It's you and me against the world.'* And on top of working her day job, she'd eat a peanut butter and jelly sandwich in the car as she rushed off to her night job as a cocktail waitress, working until 11:00 p.m. at night. It was taking me a lot longer to start making money than I had expected... so much so that Christine sold her car, downgrading from a BMW that her father bought her, to a 12-year old economy car with over 103,000 miles on it. She did this because we needed the cash to pay rent one month. She never complained... not once," Joseph explained.

Joseph smiled as he reminisced about *The Good Ole Days*. He wasn't the kind of person to hold back expressing his emotions. His eyes were filled with sentimental thoughts as he recounted the sacrifices that Christine had made for him.

She was the motivating force behind Joseph's drive.

Sure she was a cheerleader in college, but she was also a real-life cheerleader for her husband too.

And she was more than just that.

Christine believed in Joseph before Joseph even believed in himself. It was that kind of undying loyalty that I wanted in my future marriage. It was that kind of belief that could overcome all odds – the kind of belief that made miracles possible.

"Christine's father just about killed me when he found out that his daughter was the one supporting her husband, financially. He told me that I wasn't a *real man*. He told me that Christine deserved better than that, and those words ate away at me because to a certain degree, I knew he was right. It made me feel like a loser coming home everyday from the office with nothing to show for my long hours," Joseph said.

And just as he said that, Christine walked into the room.

"But you DID have something to show for your efforts, honey! You were building the foundation of your career, building your skillsets and building your sales pipeline," Christine objected.

I was shocked that Christine knew what a *sales pipeline* was. As the conversation progressed, it became obvious that Christine wasn't just Joseph's *cheerleader*.

She was his *co-pilot*.

The more we talked, the more I learned about Christine.

It wasn't easy for her in the beginning of their marriage, especially because of her father. She had grown up relatively affluent – not wealthy, but affluent.

Christine was *Daddy's Little Girl*, and when her father didn't accept Joseph, she made a choice.

Her *Us Against The World* belief even applied to her relationship with her own father. It must not have been easy for her to go against her father, siding with Joseph. She was only 21-years old when she and Joseph married, and for a young girl to go against her father's wishes… well, that took guts.

She wouldn't allow her father to talk down to Joseph, at least not in her presence. And so when her father relentlessly put Joseph down, she disassociated herself from him. Under her rules, no one was going to put down her husband… not even her own father. But even with her guts-of-steel, Christine downplayed her role, giving the credit back to Joseph.

"My husband has always been so hard on himself, Vincent. I don't know if it was harder on him to feel like he wasn't successful soon enough, or if it was harder on me knowing that he felt this way. I've always been proud of Joseph, not for the success he's achieved today, but for the effort and commitment that he had in the beginning. Those were *The Good Ole Days*. Working two jobs was easy for me. Sure it was a lot of hours, but working *hard*, for me, was *easy*. Joseph is the one that had to build something out of nothing. I could never do that. It's just not in me. Sometimes I feel bad about that, feeling like I don't deserve to be with such a visionary like Joseph," Christine confessed.

"Vincent, don't believe a word she says!" Joseph exclaimed. "Everyone has always given me all the credit and accolades for our success, but without Christine as my co-pilot, our plane would have crashed and burned. We lived in a crappy one-bedroom apartment for the first two years of our marriage. We ate *Top Ramen* noodles for dinner practically every night. On special occasions, we'd go out to dinner at this little Chinese restaurant around the corner from our apartment, and we'd split one main dish, because that's all we could afford. Do you know how much it killed me to not be able to do more for my wife? But she hung in there with me because…"

"Because I believed in him, Vincent. Joseph gives me all this credit for hanging in there with him from the beginning, but it was never a big deal to me. That's just what a *real woman* does for her man. I don't care about getting any sort of credit. I've always just wanted Joseph to shine... to be the *man* of our family. I knew that was important to him, and so it became important to me too. That's what marriage is all about – wanting something for the love of your life because it's important to *them*. Both Joseph and I are *givers* in our relationship, and when two *givers* get together, they can create magic," said Christine.

Joseph then leaned over to me, and said ever so softly, "And that's what I have with Christine. Magic."

Chapter Ten
The Beginning Of The Beginning

I woke up the following morning feeling like I was part of something bigger than me. Seeing Joseph in his home interacting with Christine and his kids gave me a more complete vision of what I really wanted in my own life.

As I walked into the office at 6:38 a.m., Joseph saw me and immediately called me into his office.

"Vincent, we'll have lunch together today. Come grab me right before noon," Joseph said.

"Sounds good," I replied.

I spent the morning making cold calls and actually booked three appointments with some investment prospects. Booking three appointments in a 4-hour block of time was pretty good. I had made huge improvements in my communication skillsets.

When lunchtime came, I walked over to Joseph's office. He told me that we'd be having lunch at *The Hotel 100*.

It's funny because even though I had been working there for the past six months with Francisco, it never crossed my mind to eat there.

As we sat down at the table and browsed the menu, I quickly realized why I'd never thought to eat at *The Hotel 100*.

It was EX-PEN-SIVE.

I guess Joseph could tell that I was intimidated by the right side of the menu, so he reassured me that lunch was on him. He insisted that I order the Maine lobster salad, ordering for the both of us.

We talked a lot about what I'd learned during my internship, and I could tell that he was proud of me, and not in a condescending way. He was really enthused about the progress I had made. I think it reminded him of his own experience in the beginning stages of his career with The Icon.

"Vincent, you've been interning at the firm for six and a half months, right?" Joseph assumptively asked.

"Yes, sir," I replied.

"And you've passed your insurance licensing exam, your Series 66 and Series 7, correct?" Joseph assumptively asked.

"Yes, sir," I replied again.

"Okay, well that does it. You've completed your internship," Joseph said to me as he stood up to firmly shake my hand.

"Joseph, thank you so much for everything you've done for me. This has been an incredible experience. I've learned so much," I said to him.

Part of me felt accomplished, yet the bigger part of me was scared to death. If my internship was over, what did that mean?

Was this the end of The Icon's deal with me?

"So Vincent, I know you've learned a lot during your internship at the firm. Have you thought much about where you want to take your career now that this is all over?" Joseph asked.

That question put a major lump in my throat.

And just as my dry throat attempted to swallow, up walked The Icon. "Look at these two power players here!" The Icon exclaimed, patting each of us on the shoulder.

I was definitely not a *power player*, but I must admit, even though The Icon was just saying that to make me feel good, it actually *did* make me feel good.

"I was just telling Vincent that his internship at the firm is now completed, and that he was a great intern," Joseph told The Icon.

"So how has this 6-month project been for you?" The Icon asked me.

I don't know what happened, but right when he said that, tears started streaming down my face.

It was over.

I was so grateful for what I had learned, but now I realized it was time for me to go out into the real world and start a real career.

The difference however, was that for the first time in my life, I knew I was prepared. I was ready to take on the world. I'd developed the ability to connect with people. I could now take complex concepts and distill them down into digestible ideas. I now, for the first time in my life, had a clear vision of what I wanted in my life.

"Sir, I've learned so much from you, Joseph and Francisco. This experience has changed my life. I'll never be the same. I don't know exactly what kind of career I should pursue, but I know this time around that I'm going to be successful because of everything you've taught me," I graciously explained, fighting to hold back more tears.

I was so grateful.

The Icon said, "Vincent, I'm glad you feel that way, and I can tell that you WILL be successful at whatever career you take on. Do me a favor. Stop by and say goodbye to Francisco before you leave, okay? Joseph and I have to stay behind and discuss a new project."

Joseph stood up and said, "Vincent, you were the best intern I've ever had. You're going to do great in whatever you do."

As I walked out of the restaurant, Francisco appeared. It was apparent that he knew that I would no longer be working under his wing at the hotel.

"Mr. Vincent. So this is it, my friend," Francisco said.

As I extended my hand to shake his, he looked at me and said, "Mr. Vincent, I think we're better friends than that by now, are we not?" Francisco gave me the warmest of hugs, as if we were brothers.

He then said, "Mr. Vincent, let me buy you a farewell cup of coffee."

Francisco ushered me into one of the private dining rooms as a gentleman was waiting for us there with coffee steeping in a French press.

"So I understand you dined at Mr. Icon's personal residence a few weekends ago," Francisco inquired.

"Yes, I did," I replied.

"Mrs. Icon is quite the lady, is she not?" Francisco stated.

I concurred, "She was amazing."

Francisco smiled. I could tell that the thought of Isabella surfaced feelings of nostalgia within him.

"You know, when Mr. and Mrs. Icon first met, I was living with Mr. Icon, along with my brothers and sister. She was always so gracious and open with us. When they decided to get married, I just assumed that I would get my own place and have my brothers and sister live with me, but she insisted that we all stay. She treated us like we were her own children. They eventually had a daughter together, but Mr. and Mrs. Icon never treated us any different. We were all one big happy family," Francisco explained.

I imagined the dynamics within this very unconventional family, and how fate had brought them together.

I envisioned the roles that both The Icon and Isabella so brilliantly filled, and the impact they made on Francisco's family.

It made it difficult not to believe in divine intervention.

As we finished our coffee, I thanked Francisco for not only teaching me so much about customer service, but for sharing so much about his personal life with me. He was so open and transparent with me. And as much as I'd like to feel special, I got the feeling that he was open and transparent with everyone, because that's the kind of person Francisco was.

He was a beautiful soul that had been through so many struggles in his life, yet he had a warmth and depth to him that you just don't find in people.

Francisco was special.

He leaned forward in his chair and said, "Mr. Vincent, you have come a long way in the last six months. Mr. Icon was right about you. You're one of the great ones. Congratulations."

Confused, I replied, "What do you mean congratulations?"

He smiled and said, "Don't tell me. You don't know?"

"Know what?" I asked, dumbfounded.

And just as those words left my mouth, The Icon and Joseph walked in, laughing hysterically.

"Vincent! Congratulations! We'd like to offer you a position at the firm as a Financial Advisor!" Joseph gushed.

I just about swallowed my tongue right there.

Here, I thought this was the end of my journey with The Icon. But on the contrary, it was just the beginning.

By the gregarious laughter coming from The Icon, Joseph and Francisco, I could tell that this announcement was all planned out. Perhaps this was my initiation into the club – scaring me half to death that they were kicking me out of the nest – and then adopting me back into the family.

"Listen, Vincent. You're going to start out as a Junior Advisor, working with Michael, one of Joseph's rising superstars," The Icon said.

I had seen Michael in the office several times, and I knew he was positioned as an up-and-coming hotshot at the firm. Michael was cocky, but walked with a swagger quite different than Joseph's or The Icon's. He was polished, but something seemed a bit off about his aura.

Nonetheless, I was thankful for the opportunity to continue my journey with The Icon.

Joseph chimed in saying, "Vincent, I need to know if you're ready for this. You're going to have to work even harder than you did as an intern. And you'd be on straight commission with no base salary, and no benefits. Everything, in terms of compensation, is based on merit and production. Are you prepared to handle that?"

"Yes, sir," I responded.

The Icon interjected, saying, "Vincent, if you want, you can keep your part-time job here at the hotel on the weekends. It may come in handy to pay your bills during the first few months."

"Thank you so much. I appreciate that option... I really do. But if it's okay with you, I'd like to respectfully decline that generous option. I feel that if I'm going to make it at the firm, I can't have a backup plan. I've got a little bit of money saved up, and three credit cards that I can use to float me for the first three months. I really want to put 100% into this... that is, if it's okay with you," I pleaded.

"The kid has guts!" Joseph exclaimed as he smiled enthusiastically at The Icon.

The Icon concurred, putting his hand on my shoulder, saying, "Vincent. That's why I believe in you. You've got an all-in type of personality. I was going to wait to teach you *Rule Number Eleven*, but I can see that you already know it. *Rule Number Eleven: Burn your ships*."

I must have looked befuddled, because The Icon started laughing hysterically.

"I'm sure there's a deep lesson embedded in that statement, but would you mind elaborating on that for me?" I said with a confident tone.

"Absolutely," said The Icon.

I listened intently as he told me the story of Hernando Cortez, the Spanish Conquistador and conqueror.

The Icon explained, "In 1519, Spanish Conquistador Hernando Cortez landed on the shores of the Yucatan in Mexico, with his army. The goal: To destroy the Aztecs and seize their treasures. Cortez, like you Vincent, had an all-in type of personality. Now, you want to talk about being a great leader, Cortez led more than 500 soldiers and 100 sailors to leave their families behind, and sail from Spain to Mexico, to overtake the Aztecs. He led a fleet of eleven ships."

I remember learning about the Aztecs in history class back in high school. I said, "Weren't the Aztecs like the most powerful empire at that time?"

"Yes. In fact, the Aztecs ruled for over 600 years. But my man Cortez... this guy was no joke. You see, what made Cortez such a great leader was that he had the ability to get 100% buy-in from his people, because he led by example. His belief system was so strong, that it became contagious. It was all or nothing with Cortez. And in this particular conquest, it was destroy the Aztecs, or be destroyed," The Icon explained.

He continued, "When Cortez landed on the shores of the Yucatan, he gathered his men together and explained to them his game plan, which was summed up in three simple words: *Burn the ships.*"

"What?" I shockingly interjected.

"Cortez literally told his men to burn the eleven ships they arrived in. Here was his philosophy: We either take the Aztecs or we die trying, but we will not give up and retreat back home. Now, at first, his men freaked out. *'Burn the ships!'* Cortez repeated. Vincent, I'm telling you, Cortez was a man after my own heart," The Icon said.

I smiled, perhaps because I knew what The Icon was getting at. He was likening burning the ships to burning bridges.

I remembered seeing a quote in a frame hanging on the wall in Joseph's office that read, *"The greatest pleasure in life is burning bridges that lead to a life of mediocrity, and accomplishing things that other people said you could not do."*

The Icon continued recounting the story of Hernando Cortez, speaking louder and louder, as I could see him becoming more and more passionate about the whole idea of burning the ships.

"And so Cortez's men burned the ships, and when they did, they morphed into more than just an army. They became obsessed believers. You see, that's what it takes to become as successful as Joseph here," as The Icon pointed towards his protégé-turned-superstar.

"From the very beginning, Joseph was obsessed. I mean, the guy stalked me in the lobby of my own office, trailed me into the elevator with a $300 bottle of tequila, and by the time we reached the first floor, he'd convinced me to go to lunch with him. He was obsessed, just like Cortez. Just like you. That's why I believe in you. That's why I know you'll be successful," The Icon said.

Hearing The Icon utter these words gave me the confidence I needed to believe. I didn't believe in myself yet, but I believed in The Icon, and if he said he believed in me, that's all I needed to hear.

I burned my ship at the hotel, respectfully of course, and went all-in at the firm.

For the next three months, I would get into the office no later than 5:00 a.m. to dial the East Coast, which was three hours ahead of me. I'd dial that phone until I built up a callous on the tip of my dialing finger. I wouldn't take a lunch break, eating at my desk as I continued to dial.

I had booked more appointments with prospective clients in a month than any other advisor ever had, shattering the firm's record, which was previously held by Joseph himself.

At 6:00 p.m., when most of the advisors headed home, I kept dialing until 8:00 p.m., attempting to reach prospective clients in Hawaii, which were three hours behind my time zone in California.

I wouldn't touch emails until the end of the day, after 8:00 p.m., because I didn't want to use up valuable time during the day where I could reach prospective clients.

I'd answer emails and develop my client proposals from 8:00 p.m. until 10:00 p.m. By this time, I'd be the only one left in the office.

I'd drink protein shakes for dinner, because I could drink them and work at the same time. And from 10:00 p.m. to midnight, I'd practice my sales pitch in the conference room.

I had heard rumors of Joseph keeping this exact schedule when he first started out, and so I figured I'd strategically follow in his footsteps, using his journey as the blueprint for my success.

One of the most valuable lessons I learned was to model myself after those I aspired to be like, and to ONLY take advice from those I aspired to be like.

I always found it interestingly ironic that so many people want to give you advice about things they've never done and about things they've never accomplished. They'll tell you about all of their perceived pitfalls in an arena that they know absolutely nothing about.

I've only been criticized for working too hard by people that weren't incredibly successful. I've only been criticized for being too obsessively driven by people that haven't accomplished much in their career. And I've only been made fun of for dreaming so big by people that didn't have the lifestyle that I aspired to create for myself and my future family.

Joseph had filled the role for me that my brother Derek once did. He had accomplished what I had always dreamed about accomplishing, and he got there not because he was born with some sort of special advantage. He got there because he was willing to work harder than everyone else, and sacrifice more than everyone else.

But my relationship with my brother was different.

I loved my brother Derek – *idolized* him, actually. But deep down, I knew that I could never accomplish what Derek did. He was born with athletic talents that 99.9% of the population was not.

Sure, Derek worked hard and trained obsessively, but things came easy to him. He was born with special God-given athletic abilities. He was incredibly talented, but he was also *gifted*.

There's a distinct difference between the two.

With a lot of hard work and dedication, you can build *talent*... but to be *gifted*... well, that you have to be born with.

What encouraged me most about Joseph's story was that it was easier for me to relate to than Derek's. With Joseph, his success seemed attainable to me, given my fortunate association with The Icon.

Joseph never attempted to *impress* me with his success.

Instead, he attempted to *inspire* me with it.

He inspired me to aspire to reach the level he had reached – to accomplish what he had accomplished – and he taught me every little nuance of his operating methodology.

I became an insatiable student of Joseph and I attempted to emulate his every move. The Icon not only mentored Joseph to get him to where he is today, but he also put his faith in Joseph to get me to the next level.

Joseph constantly reminded me that if he could do it, then so could I. He created a bond with me by continually talking about what was going through his mind when his career was in the same stage as mine.

He would tell me about his frustrations, his insecurities and his struggles when he was first starting out. And he let me know that even with all of his imperfections, that success was inevitable because he followed The Icon's system.

The word *mentor* is a term that is too loosely thrown around now days in my opinion. A *mentor* is not just a successful person that you *aspire* to be like. It's not just a successful person that *encourages* you, giving you a pep talk here and there.

A *true* mentor is someone that is magnificently successful at a level that you dream about achieving, that teaches you the EXACT step-by-step process of how they did it. Otherwise, without the exact step-by-step process, they're nothing more than an encouraging cheerleader.

What both The Icon and Joseph did for me was give me an exact process to follow that you could quantify. And when I really thought about it, what bonded me to Joseph the most was the fact that we shared one major thing in common.

We were both underdogs.

Chapter Eleven
Pecan Pie

There was one thing I knew.

I could outwork just about anybody.

Sure, a lot of people were smarter than me, more experienced than me, and more talented than me. But I knew I could work harder than everyone else, and that's exactly what I did.

Michael, who was supposed to be my Senior Manager at the firm, thought I was crazy. I was grinding it out twice as hard as he was, which made me lose respect for him. I never understood how these so-called *manager* types could expect their people to respect them when they didn't lead by example.

I watched Michael attempt to schmooze Joseph, kissing his butt constantly, but never really grinding it out like I was.

He was cocky, but in a slightly disrespectful way. It wasn't the relaxed confidence that Joseph and The Icon embodied.

Michael was more *veneer*.

He didn't have the depth of character that Joseph had. He said all the right things, and on the surface, he looked like the perfect poster boy, but I could tell he wasn't the real deal.

I could also tell that he was threatened by me.

He wanted to be the next Joseph – the next Andrei – the next Francisco. It was obvious, and I must admit, he WAS obsessed. But the difference was that to me, it seemed like he was always trying to shortcut everything. He wanted to be successful, but for all the wrong reasons.

For Michael, working with Joseph was merely a means to an end, whereas for me, I understood that the *process* was more important than the *pot of gold* at the end of the rainbow.

I continually reminded myself about what The Icon had told me about pursuing excellence instead of pursuing money.

Michael was a terrible role model for me in this area, however I refused to let him get me sidetracked.

But that was easier said than done.

I knew that my career wouldn't bring me riches overnight, but my dad would constantly send me disempowering emails about how stupid I was to pursue a commission-based career.

And there I was, nine months into this adventure, and I hadn't made a dime at the firm yet. I knew my dad was wrong, but my numbers certainly appeared to prove him right.

In my heart of hearts, I was positive that I would succeed with Joseph and The Icon, but I was running out of money faster than I had anticipated.

I thought I'd be making at least a modest income by now, but as I found out, sometimes things take a little longer to materialize than we want.

I did however have a huge prospective client that looked like they were going to do a big transaction with me worth over $60,000 in commissions.

Michael was running point on this deal, and he kept bragging to everyone about how he was going to close it. He was always bragging about stuff like this.

"It's in the bag, man! I got this! Vincent, sit back and watch my magic. Watch the pro show you how it's done... and take some good notes. You could learn a thing or two from me," said Michael.

Michael was always saying obnoxious things like this. He always made it about him, and he always communicated with a condescending tone, attempting to put other people in their place in order to make himself appear superior.

Michael was the type of guy that shamelessly congratulated himself. I think he might have even torn his rotator cuff once from patting himself on the back so hard.

I must admit, it was exciting having a big client on the hook, mostly because if the deal closed, I could make rent next month… and with a deal as big as this one, I could have paid my rent for the next 12 months.

But the client kept procrastinating, putting off making their decision until the next week… and then the next week… and then the week after that.

I had so much faith in the firm that I made the mistake of celebrating too soon before the deal had been solidified, and as the weeks dragged on, the deal eventually died on the vine.

It was devastating.

Michael blamed me, of course.

Joseph told me to brush it off, and keep grinding it out, so I did my best to stay positive.

The following week, I developed two additional opportunities, both of them even bigger than the first one. I thought to myself, "If these two deals close before the end of this month, I'll make 6-figures in my first year with the firm!"

I was sure these two deals would materialize.

It was like the excitement you have when two new rose buds begin to bloom in your in your garden in the springtime.

You see them beginning to bud… and then you see them start to bloom… and then right as they're about to blossom, the hot sun fries them to death, and they come crumbling down to the ground.

Well, that's what happened to these two prospects as well.

Michael blamed me again, of course.

And as much as I knew Michael was using me as the patsy, there was a part of me that felt responsible for losing the clients.

My old patterns of self-doubt started to run rampant, as comparisons to my brother Derek ran through my head.

Every feeling I'd ever had about not meeting other people's expectations consumed my emotions, almost as if I was reliving past failures and letdowns all over again.

I feared what The Icon thought about me – his new protégé – dropping the ball. I feared what Joseph thought about me losing three big prospective clients in a row. I feared what my father thought about my *expectations of grandeur* that were beginning to look like *delusions of grandeur*.

I walked into Joseph's office, completely defeated. He could see it written all over my face. I was frazzled, scattered, and emotionally down in the dumps.

Joseph was always incredibly busy, but no matter how busy he was, he always made time for me. I must have driven him crazy with all of my questions and interruptions, but he never made me feel like I was a nuisance.

"What's up, Vincent?" Joseph inquired.

I closed the door behind me and sat down at his desk.

"Joseph, man. I don't know what I'm doing wrong. I just screwed up two more big opportunities, and I just don't want you to lose faith in me," I said, my eyes beginning to well up with tears.

I felt like I was letting my mentor down.

Joseph stood up, walked around his massive desk, and sat down next to me.

"Vincent, there's nothing to feel ashamed about. Those two prospective clients are NOTHING!"

"But Joseph, it was THREE prospective clients," I masochistically corrected him.

"Two, three… whatever. It doesn't even matter. Vincent, do you realize how many deals I've personally lost over the course of my career? I've got a database of literally thousands of would-be clients that rejected me and my ideas. It's just part of the game, man. Don't worry about it. I'm not worried about it, so neither should you," Joseph confidently told me.

The look on my face must have told him that my burden would not be lifted quite so easily.

He started chuckling in a kind-hearted sort of way, saying, "Vincent, are you worried that I'm upset that you didn't close those deals?"

I was so embarrassed.

I couldn't even make eye contact with him.

I just nodded my head.

"Vincent, man! That's NOTHING! Forget those guys! They probably weren't going to do anything with you from day one. Sometimes prospects just yank your chain without ever intending to do a transaction with you in the first place. It happens. Look, don't focus on the ones that don't close. Just move on to the next one and don't lose focus of the fundamentals. Your entire goal shouldn't be to convince people to become clients. We're not in the *convincing game*. We're in the *identifying game*. All we're trying to do is identify who wants what we've got. If they don't want what we've got – for whatever reason – that's okay. Statistically, 70% - 80% of them aren't going to become your clients no matter what you say or do. But that also means that 20% - 30% will... and that's where we make our money," Joseph empathetically explained.

He continued, "Look Vincent, you know why I'm a multi-millionaire? I'm not a multi-millionaire because I can convince 20% - 30% of the people I meet with to become my clients. I'm a multi-millionaire because I'm willing to put up with the 70% - 80% that reject me. Not everyone can deal with rejection, so if you train yourself to be able to accept getting rejected 70% - 80% of the time, you're going to become a multi-millionaire too! Again, all you've got to do is IDENTIFY who wants what you've got. Sure, you've got to go through a lot of prospects to find them, but once you understand this law – The Law Of Large Numbers – you'll find that the most successful people in business are the ones that kept grinding it out when everyone else was quitting. In most cases, massive success is preceded by massive amounts of failure."

Joseph made things simple, which gave me clarity.

Whenever I started to doubt myself and run my old emotional patterns of self-sabotage and self-pity, Joseph had a way of helping me see things clearly.

He wasn't one of those hype men that espoused fluffy motivational fluff. He took the time to explain things in a way that made logical sense to me, implying that the road to success was simple, as long as you followed The Icon's blueprint.

The key principle he continued to reinforce with me was that based on following The Icon's rules, the road to success was *simple* – not *easy* – but *simple*.

Whenever my turbulent emotions complicated things, causing me to lose focus, Joseph reminded me that although you have to work *hard* – that nothing comes *easy* – that the process is *simple*.

I just had to religiously follow The Icon's golden set of success rules – his *life rules*.

But despite Joseph's encouragement and The Icon's unwavering faith in my potential, I still had moments of massive self-doubt.

As I drove home from the office that evening, I stopped by the drive through window at *Burger King*, entertaining the idea of treating myself to some comfort food. Whenever I felt depressed, a nice warm piece of pie always gave me a little temporary comfort.

As my car approached the parking lot, I rolled down my window, and pulled up to the illuminated menu.

It was late, around 11:00 p.m.

There were some high school students hanging out in the parking lot, eating their *Whoppers* and fries, sipping on their milkshakes, without a care in the world.

As I watched them hanging out, listening to their music booming from their car stereos, laughing and joking, I became even more depressed. In that moment, they seemed to have it all.

And in that moment, I felt alone.

As excited and grateful as I was about the opportunity to work with The Icon and Joseph, my emotions were also filled with feelings of failure.

My eyes were slowly redirected towards the illuminated drive-thru menu, as they focused in on the desert section.

Pecan pie.

$1.39.

I must have stared at that pecan pie on the menu for at least five minutes, contemplating.

Back when I was a kid, my mom used to make me pecan pie, which she knew was my favorite. Whenever she would make it, my mom would enthusiastically let me know that she made it just for me.

She'd say, "Vincent, sweetheart. I made your favorite – pecan pie – just for you honey."

My smile would beam ear to ear.

Sure I loved pecan pie, but it was more than just my favorite desert. It was something that my mom made for me that made me feel *loved*. It made me feel *special*.

And my mom knew it.

It brought her great joy to know that my tormented soul found solace in knowing that someone – my mother – took notice of something that I found pleasure in.

As I sat there in my car in the *Burger King* parking lot, staring at the illuminated drive-thru menu, focusing in on the $1.39 pecan pie, my eyes began to well up with tears. And as I contemplated whether or not I should treat myself to a piece of pecan pie, a single stream of tears from the corner of my left eye slowly trickled down my face.

Coming to the realization that I couldn't even afford to buy a lousy piece of pie for $1.39 made me feel like a total loser.

Now in reality, I could have just charged it on my credit card and paid 17.99% interest on the $1.39 piece of pie. I had already racked up a significant amount of credit card debt during my internship, so it's not like an additional $1.39 was going to bankrupt me or anything.

But in that moment, what consumed my emotions most was that I felt like I didn't *deserve* to treat myself.

It was a terrible feeling – the feeling of being undeserving of something so simple. I could feel the blood rush in behind my eyeballs, as my mouth became tense and my lips began to tremble.

In that moment, I was ashamed and embarrassed of where I was in life, financially.

Sure, I had learned invaluable lessons from Joseph and The Icon, but I hadn't achieved any significant material success yet, and despite what Joseph said about those three lost clients being *nothing*, I still felt like I was failing him.

And so I decided, after much deliberation, to forgo the $1.39 pecan pie.

As I slowly drove out of the parking lot onto Beverly Boulevard that evening, I watched the illuminated drive-thru menu vanish in my rear view mirror.

But as depressing as it was for a $1.39 expense to be outside of my budget, I distinctly remember saying to myself, "Pecan pie, we shall meet again my friend."

I had been beaten up in so many different areas of my life, I was used to it. I had built up a tolerance for rejection and failure, and perhaps that was one of the greatest outcomes I was blessed with through my struggles.

I had the ability to keep moving forward.

Sure it was emotionally painful – the feeling of failure and let down – but somehow getting knocked down never prevented me from getting back up.

That was a lesson I had learned before I even met The Icon. I truly believed that it's not how many times you fail that counts. What counts is how many times you can fail and keep moving forward, and *how* a man moves forward in life is what defines his character.

I kept telling myself that one day I would have my pecan pie, and eat it too.

It had been thirteen weeks since I had been working under Michael, failure after failure. But then it finally happened.

I landed my first client.

It was a small deal.

I only made a whopping $817 in commissions on the deal. But it wasn't the size of the client that got me fired up. It was the fact that I knew that if I acquired a client once, that I could do it again.

I felt a huge weight lifted off my shoulders. I didn't realize it until this moment, but comparatively, I felt like I had been walking around wearing a hundred-pound backpack, weighing me down. And in that moment of receiving my very first commission check, that weight was instantaneously lifted from my overwhelmingly burdened shoulders.

Michael didn't make things any easier for me though. He bragged to Joseph, as well as to every other member of the firm, that HE was the reason I closed the deal.

But even though I knew it wasn't true, I kept my mouth shut. All I cared about was moving forward.

I even developed a personal mantra.

A.M.F.

Always Moving Forward.

Despite my past failures, and despite any future failures, I was committed to always moving forward. That's what winners do, and despite my losing track record, I believed deep down that I was a *winner*.

The following week, I closed another deal.

The week after, I closed two more.

The week after that, I closed my fifth deal.

When I counted up all of my commissions in that four-week span, I'd made $13,491 in commissions, and I was on a roll.

I wanted to call my dad and tell him the good news, but I didn't. I knew better. He would surely find something negative to say about me, or what I was doing, so I decided to celebrate with the one person that I knew would understand just how excited I was.

I called The Icon.

As the phone rang, I eagerly anticipated hearing The Icon's voice, but to my surprise, Isabella answered The Icon's cell phone.

"Hola Vincent! I hear you're having a great month! Congratulations! Hold on, let me get my husband for you," she exclaimed.

"Vincent! Five new clients and thirteen grand in commissions! Man, that's awesome! I just got off the phone with Joseph. He told me you've been crushing it this month!" The Icon exclaimed.

"We're on our way to the airport – going to be in Miami for the week – but Vincent! Keep it up, kid! You're headed for the stars!" The Icon told me.

Once again, I found myself empowered.

Amazing how a two-minute phone call could have such a powerful effect on me. It also dawned on me that Isabella knew about my big month too. She seemed to be just as excited for me as The Icon. It was like she had a vested interest in me, the same way that a proud mother would.

I had lost my own mother to pancreatic cancer when I was in college. My mom was a great woman. She was my number one cheerleader. Even though she had suffered an eleven-month battle with cancer, she never complained during the entire battle.

She would always say, "The Lord has blessed me with friends that love me. He let me spend seventeen wonderful years with Derek, before He took him home to be with Him. And God has blessed me with a wonderful son in you, Vincent. I don't have any complaints. In fact, I think I'm pretty lucky."

That was my mom's perspective on life. Even in the face of a very painful illness, I only remember her smiling, never complaining.

She was grateful for her life.

Watching my mom's faith in God spill into every area of her life was inspiring. When I was a kid, it would drive me a little nuts listening to her praise the Lord for every little thing. But as an adult, in retrospect, it made me aware that I should never take anything for granted.

My mom's positive and warm spirit was special, and I missed it. I missed *her*.

In no way am I saying that Isabella replaced my mom, but she did embody a similar spirit about her.

Over the next twelve months, my fondness for Isabella grew and grew. She became a mother figure for me, something I had longed for, ever since I lost my own mom back in college. I had spent a lot of time with both her and The Icon, not only talking about business, but also about life in general.

By this time, I was doing REALLY well with the firm. That year, I made $218,483 in commissions. Each month, I was getting stronger and stronger.

By my third year at the firm, I had been promoted to *Senior Advisor*, and I was running a team of twelve Junior Advisors. I was now the mentor to my team of Juniors, just as Michael had been to me. The difference however, was that I actually *cared* about the Juniors on my team.

Michael was in it for one reason and one reason only: To make money. He never cared about his team. He treated them like pawns in his scheme to amass his personal riches.

I saw many of them quit, and I knew it had everything to do with the way he treated them. As my team grew, I watched his team shrink, and it angered him to watch me pass him.

He made every effort to bad-mouth me, claiming that the only reason I was doing so well was that I brown-nosed The Icon and Joseph.

Sure it made me angry that he always seemed to try to discredit me, but at the end of the day, it didn't matter. One thing Joseph taught me was to bury my head and work my butt off, and every six months, come up for air... check my results... and then bury my head again and keep grinding.

I had a tremendous amount of respect for Joseph. He really embodied all of the principles I'd learned from The Icon. And ironically, or perhaps not so ironically, he didn't seem to care much for Michael.

As time went on, I would hear Michael discredit Joseph behind his back, saying that Joseph was a brown-noser, accusing him of the same thing he accused me of. I'd watch Michael attempt to poison the minds of his new Junior Advisors, trying to talk-down Joseph, and attempt to take credit for things he had no business taking credit for.

But as with everything in life, eventually the truth got exposed. As I walked into the office at 5:52 a.m. one Friday morning, there were two SEC investigators at our front desk, and as I walked back to my desk on the sales floor, I saw Michael in handcuffs being escorted out by two police officers.

Michael had gotten caught for insider trading.

Chapter Twelve
What Goes Around Comes Back Around

I immediately walked towards Joseph's office, but I saw that he was in a serious meeting with our compliance officer, along with two men who I assumed were investigators.

I called The Icon from my cell phone and ducked into our conference room for privacy purposes.

"Sir, are you aware of what's going on with Michael down here at the firm?" I asked.

"Of course. It's all under control. We've been watching Michael closely for several weeks, and we suspected something fishy was going on. So we hired a private investigator and an I.T. specialist to track his trades and his whereabouts. We found out he was meeting with some corporate moles off site, and once our compliance officer caught him in the act, we made the call to the SEC... and because we were proactive and transparent with them from the very beginning, they absolved us from all liability. Michael will be facing five years in a Federal prison," The Icon reported.

What goes around comes back around.

Perhaps I shouldn't have felt this way, but I was glad Michael was going away.

He was a punk.

I actually felt guilty for not ripping his head off for talking disrespectfully about Joseph. Joseph had been like a big brother to me, and I should have told him that I'd heard Michael discrediting him.

From that moment on, I made a promise to myself that I would never let anyone at the firm talk negatively about Joseph, the firm, or The Icon. I would defend their names with vigilance.

Over the next year, from time to time, I'd occasionally hear some of the new Junior Advisors talking amongst themselves, questioning the firm's system. They'd question the firm's protocol. They'd question the sales scripts. They'd question our process of acquiring new clients.

It drove me crazy, because here they were, fresh out of college with no experience and zero track record, and yet they were questioning Joseph's directives.

These young punks were questioning the very system that was developed by The Icon himself. It baffled me how they would question principles that were proven to work by the most powerful players in the industry.

One time, I heard a group of the new Junior Advisors talking about how they didn't think the script worked, and I just lost it on them.

"Hey, are you guys a bunch of morons? How much money have you made in this industry, huh? I make more in a month than you idiots make in a year, and I follow the firm's system 100%! Who do you think you are to question ANYTHING here?" I ranted.

Just then, Joseph walked up and said, "Whoa! What's going on here guys?"

"These punks are questioning our system here. They're saying the script doesn't work. Who do you IDIOTS think you are, huh?" I yelled.

"Whoa, whoa! Vincent, take it easy. Let me talk to these guys," Joseph said.

I walked away heated.

Five minutes later, Joseph called me into his office.

As I sat down across from Joseph, I ranted, "These little punks! They don't know jack, and they're talking trash about our firm? Talking trash about you? Disrespecting you? You should fire those little punks!"

"Vincent, my man. Slow your roll. Chill out, brother. These guys are brand new. Their belief system has yet to be solidified," Joseph calmly explained.

I didn't understand why Joseph wasn't more upset.

"Look Vincent, when a new Junior Advisor starts out, they're trying to figure out if this career is for real or not. It takes them some time to figure it out," Joseph said.

I practically cut Joseph off, saying, "Come on man. The Junior Advisors on my team never say stuff like that."

"Yeah, you know why?" Joseph said. "It's because they're afraid of you. They're afraid to tell you what they're really thinking... how they really feel. I guarantee you, every night your guys go home, they're on the Internet, searching for jobs that pay base salaries."

Joseph went on to tell me that this was one of the main things I needed to improve on as a leader.

"Look, Vincent. I appreciate the fact that you're so passionate and loyal to the firm and to me. Remember I told you about the time I almost beat that guy to death that confronted The Icon in the restaurant? I had the right intentions, but there have been many roads paved to hell on good intentions. Listen, I love the fact that you're offended that anyone would talk negatively about me, but you've got to realize, it's going to happen. It comes with the territory," Joseph explained.

I countered, "Joseph, with all due respect, I never questioned you or the firm's system. I never questioned The Icon, and neither have you. These young punks shouldn't either."

Joseph smiled, saying, "Vincent, it's time you learned *Rule Number Twelve: Erase the word 'should' from your vocabulary.* People *should* do a lot of things, but they don't, and they won't."

He continued, "People *should* work harder. They *should* exercise and eat healthier. They *should* stop smoking. They *should* be more honest. The problem is that even though they *should* do these things, they *won't*. You've got to accept the fact that people are going to do whatever they're going to do. Don't expect them to do what they *should* do. You'll be setting yourself up for disappointment."

Joseph paused as if he was searching to recall something important. He then looked at me and said, "Vincent, there's a quote I want you to commit to memory. It says, '*A man convinced against his will, is of the same opinion still.*' What this means is that even if you convince someone that you're right... and even if they comply with your tyrant demands... they won't comply for very long. They'll temporarily conform to avoid your wrath, but they won't be on your team in the long run."

"So how do you get your people to do what you want them to do?" I asked.

"You can't *get* them to do anything... but you can *inspire* them by modeling the behavior you're trying to get your people to emulate... and then you've got to overtly praise the people that are following your lead, in front of everyone. Human beings generally want to please others. They also want to feel like they're part of the club. Criticizing *bad behavior* alienates them from you. Instead, focus on congratulating *good behavior*. They'll naturally seek to repeat the behavior that got noticed... that got praised. This is what you need to amplify," Joseph said.

He continued, "This is also a vetting process, because what you'll find is that the people that want to be on your team – the ones that embody your belief system – will seek to win over your approval. They'll want to walk like you... talk like you... act like you... and be like you. The ones that don't, won't. They'll easily and obviously remove themselves from your organization and your life, which is ultimately a very positive thing."

I replied, "Joseph, you make it sound so easy to do."

Joseph let out a big chuckle and said, "There's nothing easy about this. It can be a very difficult thing to do, emotionally. It'll challenge your ego. It'll make your stomach upset. It'll drive you absolutely nuts. But you've got to change the way you look at leading your people. You've got to approach your leadership role from a completely different angle, and a large part of this – perhaps the largest part of this process – is to stop expecting people to do what they *should* do."

Joseph continued, "Vincent, if I had a dime for every time one of my sales managers told me that one of our employees *should* have done something, I'd be a multi-millionaire."

I replied, "But you ARE a multi-millionaire."

Joseph smiled and said, "You see."

I got the point. I wasn't the first manager to struggle with this concept. It drove me crazy how people continually got in their own way of success.

When I met The Icon, I immediately submitted to his way of doing things because he obviously had an incredible track record. I couldn't argue with his track record, so from my perspective, I wasn't about to argue with his methods. They clearly worked. That's probably why I got so upset with these young, inexperienced Junior Advisors.

I figured they should just shut up, work hard, and follow the system. But then I caught myself. Joseph clearly had a ton of experience and a wealth of knowledge when it came to leading people, and so as much as it ticked me off that the Junior Advisors were questioning the firm's system, here I was, questioning Joseph's leadership technique.

I immediately apologized to Joseph.

Joseph put his hand on my shoulder and said, "Vincent, people like you and me... we're different. Why do you think The Icon chose us? Why do you think he chose Andrei and Francisco? I'll tell you why. It's because we're different. We're more driven. We're more loyal. We're willing to take more chances. We're willing to do what's right, instead of what's more convenient. We don't take shortcuts. We are... different."

"Joseph, I get what you're saying, but if we can be these things, why can't all of our Junior Advisors?" I asked in frustration.

"It's not that they *can't*. It's that they *choose* not to. Trust me Vincent, I understand what you're saying. I used to feel the exact same way you're feeling right now. But what The Icon taught me regarding this issue has been one of the most valuable lessons I've learned thus far. He taught me that as a leader, you can't force someone to believe. You can't force someone to have faith. Faith is a choice," Joseph told me.

"So how do you deal with these Junior Advisors that are still questioning everything?" I asked.

"You need to lead by example. That's the difference between being a *manager,* versus being a *leader.* Managers *manage*, and no one wants to follow a *manager*. No one gets fired up about being *managed*. But if you exemplify everything this firm stands for – everything The Icon stands for – the right Junior Advisors will bond with you. They'll want to be just like their leader. You'll become a magnet for the right type of Advisors... the type of Advisors we want here. The ones that don't want to be like you, well, they'll quit. The system will spit them out. And that's okay. They have the right to choose another career path," said Joseph.

"You mean they have the right to be dumb, broke and unsuccessful, and go get a cruddy cubicle job with some company that could care less about their future!" I exclaimed.

"Well, you and I might believe that, because we've been around the block to know how special this opportunity is, but these young guys... they don't. Some of them are going to have to go out there and see for themselves how cruddy the cubicle route is, working for a company where no one cares about them," Joseph said in a slightly somber tone.

"You mean that because they don't know any better, you can't expect them to know any better?" I asked.

"Something like that. But here's the key thing about this rule. It becomes a slippery slope when you start developing a strong conviction about what you do, which you certainly have. You see, you've got to make sure you don't start judging people that don't follow in your footsteps. That's where *Rule Number Thirteen* comes in. *Never Judge Another Person's Drive."*

"Not everyone is cut out to be an entrepreneur. It doesn't make them any less of a person than you are. They just don't want it as bad as you or I do. Take Lindsey, my assistant, for example. She's on a modest salary, relative to what you make. Her goal isn't to become filthy rich. She's content with a modest lifestyle, and there's nothing wrong with that, for her," Joseph said.

I interjected, "Joseph! Come on man. You're telling me she wouldn't rather be living in a mansion, driving a hot car, with a ton of cash in the bank?"

"Look, everyone wants to be rich. Everyone wants to have the finer things in life. But not everyone wants it bad enough to sacrifice other areas of their life, and there's nothing wrong with that. For example, look at you. You're not going to become Mr. Olympia, right? You're not in terrible shape, but you ain't rocking six pack abs either, right?" Joseph exclaimed.

"No," I sheepishly replied.

"Okay, so is it safe to say that having the physique of a Greek God isn't as important to you as having a rocking career?" Joseph asked.

"Sure, that's a fair statement," I confirmed.

"Okay, so you value your career to the point where you're not willing to give up advancing your career by spending five hours in the gym everyday like a professional bodybuilder would. Is that fair to say?" Joseph asked.

"I guess you could say that," I said.

"Okay, well Lindsey isn't judging you for that, accusing you of not being more driven to have a body like an Adonis, right?" Joseph said.

"So what does she want? Why is she working for you?" I asked Joseph.

Joseph then said, "Why don't you ask her for yourself?"

He called Lindsey into his office impromptu and put me on the spot. Lindsey walked in and said, "What can I do for you Joseph?"

"Vincent here wants to ask you something. I'm going to go walk out on the sales floor and see what's happening. Vincent, go ahead and ask Lindsey what you want to ask her," Joseph said, exiting his office.

I felt like an idiot sitting there, Lindsey looking at me with her kind eyes. I immediately felt like a judgmental jerk.

"Umm, Lindsey. I don't know how to ask you this, but… umm, why do you work for Joseph? I heard you graduated from an Ivy League School, and… umm…" I stuttered and stammered.

"You mean what's an Ivy League grad doing working as an assistant making only $38,000 a year?" Lindsey asked. The side of her mouth curled up, as if she knew she was making me feel uncomfortable.

"Lindsey, I didn't mean it like that," I defended myself.

"Sure you did," Lindsey said smiling. "It's okay. I don't take offense to that. You see Vincent, I've worked for other employers, and made almost double what I make here. But the reason I love my job here is that Joseph treats me with respect. I've even gotten to know Mr. Icon, and as rich and powerful as he is, he makes me feel special here, like I'm part of something. I've got friends that make more than me, but they hate going to work. I, on the other hand, *love* coming to work. Who knows, one day, maybe I'll become a Financial Advisor here, and make even more money than you! But for now, I'm just happy to be part of this team."

I realized what Joseph was trying to teach me about those Junior Advisors that drove me crazy. Everyone wants something different. For some, it's conservative stability, like my father. For some, it's having a mentor, like Joseph. And for some, like Lindsey, it was feeling like she was part of something bigger than herself. She didn't even care about her rank on this team. She didn't care that she wasn't the star or the team captain. She just wanted to be on the team.

That encounter with Lindsey would later give me greater insight into how to be a better leader to my Junior Advisors. I wanted to make over $1 million a year, while some of my guys only wanted to make a couple hundred thousand… and some only wanted to break the six-figure mark.

To be honest, some of them would have been happy just to make forty grand a year, but to do it at a firm where they felt like they were part of something.

Who was I to judge what another person's aspirations were? The more I thought about it, I was sure there were people in this world that made $20 million a year that looked at me and said to themselves, "What's wrong with this slacker? How could he be happy with only making a crappy million bucks a year?"

Everything is relative, especially when it comes to money.

The lessons never stopped coming, and I openly embraced every one of them... even the ones that made me realize the errors of my ways.

The next year seemed to fly by.

I had earned several promotions and was now Vice-President of the firm. Joseph had taught me to not only be a top Financial Advisor, but he had also groomed me to be a leader and a businessman.

I was now Joseph's right-hand man at the firm, second in command.

Things were really looking up, and I was grateful.

Chapter Thirteen
New York, New York

By this time, I had gotten to know Joseph and his family very well. He was more that just a mentor to me. He had become my closest friend.

He had followed The Icon's blueprint for success to the Nth degree. Joseph's wife was amazing. His kids were excellent students and star athletes.

He was living *The Great Life*.

I felt fortunate to learn from Joseph on a daily basis, but my gratitude towards him extended far beyond him teaching me how to manage investment portfolios and lead my sales team. He taught me how to be a better man, and he led me by example, just as The Icon had done for him – just as The Icon had done for me.

My social life mostly revolved around spending time with The Icon and Isabella, and with Joseph and his family. Sure I went out with a handful of girls, but I actually enjoyed my time with these two families more than I did living the single life.

I would play *Legos* with Joseph's kids, building tractors and different kinds of trucks. His kids got such a kick out of building things with me, then destroying them, laughing as they pretended to crash them into each other.

This was the life I desired.

Don't get me wrong. Dating was fun too.

It's amazing what the dating world was like, once I had confidence and money. Some of the girls I dated were models and aspiring actresses. Some were socialites. But in the end, none of them had any substance.

During that time in my life, romantic relationships were not my primary focus. I was on a mission to take my career to the next level. I remembered what The Icon had told me about being obsessed with success, and how in the early stages of your career, obsession was a requirement.

Well, to me, I was still in the early stages of my career.

I had many dinners with The Icon and Isabella, many of them at their home. But one was especially interesting.

The Icon manned the grill as usual, as Isabella and I socialized with Joseph and Christine.

When it came time to eat, The Icon only ate steamed vegetables – funky vegetables – like kale and Brussels sprouts. He then opened about seven different bottles of different types of vitamins, mostly herbs.

"Yeah, I know it's weird, but I'm on this new diet kick. I'm juicing in the morning, and I'm on this funky organic plant-based program. I've been doing this for about a week now, and I'm feeling great!" The Icon said.

As the rest of us ate delicious grilled chicken and carne asada, The Icon remained disciplined, eating his steamed veggies. The Icon always impressed me with his discipline.

Then Christine put me on the spot.

"So Vincent, Joseph tells me you're seeing a new girl. How's it going?" she inquired, egging me on.

"It's alright," I responded, with little enthusiasm.

"That's it? You don't sound too excited about her," she said.

Joseph jumped in, saying, "That's because he had *The New Girlfriend Talk* with her."

"What's *The New Girlfriend Talk?*" she inquired.

I said, "*The New Girlfriend Talk* is where I tell the girl that my primary focus is my business, and that she shouldn't expect any lavish gifts, luxury vacations, or any of the normal foo-foo stuff. My entire life right now is focused on building my empire."

Christine gasped.

And at that moment, Isabella rushed to my defense. "Hey, Vincent's future wife will appreciate this. Isn't that right Vincent?"

"That's right!" I enthusiastically confirmed.

Isabella got it. She understood my mindset.

And how could she not?

She was married to The Icon.

She understood the importance of building the foundation of a business, because she was part of The Icon's journey.

She knew what it took.

It became so clear to me in that moment that if I were to ever get married again, it would have to be to a woman that *got it* the way Isabella *got it*.

"Vincent, you keep focusing on building your foundation. When the time is right, the right woman will appear. Always remember to never accept anything less than what you deserve, especially when it comes to choosing a wife," Isabella said.

And immediately following those words of wisdom, The Icon and Joseph high-fived each other. By the reaction it elicited from my two mentors, it was obvious that they agreed with Isabella.

Then Christine asked, "Is *The New Girlfriend Talk* really that necessary?"

I looked at Isabella, hoping she would come to my defense again, but Joseph beat her to the punch.

"Honey, I never had to have *The New Girlfriend Talk* with you because you were on board from the very beginning. You *got it*. Girls nowadays expect to be wined and dined 24-7 like they're freakin' princesses," said Joseph.

Had I not spent time with Joseph and Christine, I wouldn't have bought that explanation, but having gotten to know Christine and the role she played in their marriage, I knew Christine *got it*.

In fact, she *got it* so much that she couldn't fathom a woman *not* getting it. That part of Christine always put a smile on my face. She didn't understand *The New Girlfriend Talk* because she never had to receive it.

At the end of dinner, The Icon gathered all of us together in his living room, and poured everyone a small sifting glass of the *Frida Kahlo* tequila I had given him four years ago, finishing off the last bit of it.

"I would like to propose a toast," he announced. "Vincent has been with us now for over four years, and he's proven himself to be a sensational Financial Advisor... he's grown to become a fantastic leader, thanks to Joseph's mentorship at the firm... and he's become a great friend... part of our family."

The Icon's voice quivered slightly, and his eyes became a bit glassy.

"Oh, honeyeeeeeee!" Isabella said, as she held his hand. She looked at me and said, "My husband gets so sentimental about things like this. He has grown to really love you Vincent."

Regaining his composure, The Icon continued, "And I'd like to announce the expansion of our firm, and the opening of our New York City office!"

The room erupted in applause.

"Hold on, hold on. But that's not the best part. The best part is that I'd like to announce my new Managing Partner, who will be running this new office. Vincent, we're counting on you to spearhead this project and lead the charge. Congratulations!" The Icon exclaimed, hugging me like we had just won the Super Bowl.

I was floored.

"Oh my God. I... I... I don't know what to say," I said as The Icon and Joseph enjoyed the announcement the way a proud parent basks in the glow of their child's accomplishment.

The wives were obviously happy for me too, celebrating my promotion, and the men – The Icon, Joseph and myself – became even more bonded in that moment.

I had officially become part of the club.

I think the emotions that I shared with The Icon and Joseph that night were emotions that only an accomplished, driven man can appreciate.

It's an acknowledgement of all your hard work – your life's work – that ultimately defines your ability to provide for your family.

I was now part of a legendry team – a legendary *family*.

And so I was New York City bound.

The Icon instructed me that Joseph would fly out the following month to help me set things up, but that initially, Andrei would help me get established in the city.

Andrei had permanently moved to New York to oversee the jewelry company that he built with The Icon.

When I arrived in New York, there stood Andrei to greet me as I deboarded the plane. He approached me, giving me a big hug, saying, "Protégé turned Superstar! Welcome to the family!"

Andrei seemed completely different.

Sure, he still had his Eastern European swagger, but he seemed so much more approachable.

When I asked him about it, he explained, "Hey bro, when I first met you almost five years ago at the coffee shop, I didn't know who the f*** you were. With me, you gotta prove yourself before I let you into my circle. I get real protective of The Icon when a new face comes along. I've seen him get burned before. You saw it with that f***ing punk Michael at the firm, right?"

"Yeah, I saw that coming, actually. I never liked that guy," I said.

Andrei confirmed, "I never met him, but Joseph told me about him. If it was up to me, I would have dumped him off the f***in' Santa Monica pier with cement shoes."

Even though Andrei said it with a smirk, I got the feeling that he was only half-kidding.

But Andrei always spoke highly of Joseph. He clearly had a lot of respect for Joseph, even though his lifestyle was completely different.

Andrei was single, and loved to mingle. He didn't seem to have much interest in any long-term relationships, and marriage was the last thing on his mind.

"Vincent, I'm gonna to be your wingman out here in NYC, and I'm gonna hook you up with all the right people. Rollin' with me is gonna make you a f***in' celebrity out here. You'll see," Andrei confidently boasted.

One thing Andrei didn't lack was confidence.

"You're gonna to stay at *The Hotel 100*, right in the middle of Times Square, until you get set up with a more permanent pad," Andrei explained.

"I didn't realize The Icon had a hotel in New York," I said, mildly stunned.

"Bro, whatchu live in a f***in' closet or something? The Icon has *Hotel 100s* in Beverly Hills, New York City, Miami, Honolulu, and he's talkin' about opening another one in Panama City," Andrei told me.

He continued, "Look here bro, you're gonna work like a machine during the day, and you're gonna party like a f***in' rockstar with me at night."

Andrei was a free spirit. He embodied the work-hard-play-hard lifestyle, and was always talking about a new restaurant opening or a new club opening. He was definitely connected in the club scene.

I would end long days at the office wrapping up around 10:00 p.m., and I'd get a call from Andrei wanting to go out. I always accepted his offers and I must admit, it was fun.

He'd always walk to the front of the line, and the doormen would always greet him, ushering us to a private table. It was like he was a celebrity in this world.

One night, we had a late dinner and a few cocktails at a swanky new restaurant in Tribeca. The crowd was a *who's who* of

New York. I think Andrei and I were the only ones there that weren't movie stars or supermodels.

"Andrei, long time my friend. You're dressed like a million bucks as always," said a soft spoken, distinguished man as he shook Andrei's hand.

"Bobby! Great to see you, man. How'd your wife like that diamond necklace we did for her?" Andrei inquired.

"Oh man, she LOVED it. She wore it to my movie premier last month. It looked insane on the red carpet," the gentleman replied.

"It was sick, right? I saw you guys there. She looked f***in' amazing. And you... you were brilliant in that film, man. You crushed it," Andrei complimented.

"Thanks buddy. Marty did a great job. This might be his best work, ever. It reminded me of *The Good Ole Days... The Good Fella Days*. I think we might both get nominations this year," said the gentleman.

"Well, you deserve it Bobby. Really, you do," Andrei confirmed.

"I appreciate the vote of confidence Andrei. Listen, I've got to run, but can your guy hook me up with Massimo again? I need a new line up of suits for some events I have coming up," the gentleman asked.

"Of course, anything for you Bobby. You know that. Just have your publicist hit me up on my private cell number, and I'll put her in touch with my guy, personally," Andrei confidently reassured him.

"Thanks Andrei," he said.

"Oh, Bobby... this is my good friend Vincent. The Icon's opening up a New York office for his wealth management firm, and Vincent is the big shot that's gonna be running the show out here," Andrei boasted.

"Hi Vincent, it's a pleasure to meet you. I'm Robert," the gentleman warmly said, introducing himself.

"Fellas, I've gotta run. Vincent, if you're with The Icon and Andrei, you're with the right people, but I'm sure you already know that. Andrei, I'll have my publicist call you about the suits," he said as he departed, making his way through the restaurant, signing a few autographs.

Star-struck, I said, "Andrei, was that…"

"Yup."

"And when he was talking about Marty, was he talking about Martin…"

"Yup."

"How the heck do you know Robert…"

"He's a client of mine. He's introduced me to some pretty big time clients out here. These guys drop some serious dough on bling. If you want your lady to be dripping in ice, I'm the guy out here. I'm *The Ice Man*," Andrei said.

Just then, three incredibly sexy girls approached us, slithering up from behind us like serpents. There was a Brazilian girl that stood almost six-feet tall, partially because she was wearing 5-inch stilettos.

She had long dark, straight hair that effortlessly flowed down her open-backed sequin halter-top… as her micro-mini skirt barely covered her perfect derrière, exposing her longer-than-life bronze legs.

The other two supermodels were blonde Australian twins that fully embodied the term *blonde bombshells.*

Their perfectly sun-kissed skin looked as though they sunbathed in the nude for a living. These girls were beyond *hot*.

"Hi Andrei," the tall, sultry Brazilian girl whispered in his ear, as the two additional bombshells followed her like a *Baywatch Entourage*. These girls looked like they stepped right out of a *Sports Illustrated Swimsuit Issue* photo shoot.

"Sweetheart, give me and my boy Vincent a few minutes to catch up, and come back around in about 10 minutes. Can you do that for me?" Andrei said nonchalantly.

"Oh… umm, okay," she said, a bit taken aback.

Andrei winked at me.

As Andrei so casually put the these three supermodels in a holding tank, I asked him, "Dude, are you nuts? Why'd you shoo them away?"

"Bro, they'll be back. Trust me. I got it like that," Andrei said, as if it was nothing.

"Who are those girls?" I asked.

"The Brazilian one with the long dark hair – the one that whispered in my ear – she was *Miss Maxim* last year. The other two are just a couple of her lingerie model friends," Andrei said, unimpressed.

As I attempted to pick my jaw up off the ground, Andrei could tell I was still in a state of supermodel shock.

"Alright Vincent. Time to learn *Rule Number Fourteen: Whoever is willing to walk away first, has the power,*" Andrei said, in his overly confident voice.

"You see all these schmoes here tonight? These guys are gonna be staring at our chicks all night. They're gonna put them up on a pedestal, and tell them how beautiful they are… and you know what? Our chicks ain't gonna be interested one bit. None of these guys have the guts to send these chicks away like I just did. And you know who else saw me send them away? Every single chick in this place. They just saw me brush off the three hottest chicks in here. You know what that makes me in their eyes? The mother f***in' man! King Kong ain't got sh** on me, bro," Andrei boasted.

It took a lot to impress Andrei, and in his world – *The World Of Andrei* – supermodels were a dime a dozen. And just as Andrei had fully expected, ten minutes later, the three girls returned, as Andrei graciously gave them permission to join us.

These girls were actually *grateful* to share a table with us.

Imagine that.

I could tell that by rolling with Andrei, my social life was about to be upgraded… dramatically.

Andrei had adapted well to the New York City lifestyle. I think the East Coast vibe was more in line with Andrei's vibe. He lived for the nightlife, and NYC had some of the best nightlife you could get.

Andrei certainly had the lay of the land in NYC, and his bachelor pad was a bachelor pad of all bachelor pads – a penthouse right on Park Avenue.

The first time I saw Andrei's *Park Avenue* penthouse, it was at a private cocktail party he hosted at his home for a few of his high-end diamond clients. These were the kind of clients that made professional athletes look broke.

They were famous movie producers, owners of major fashion magazines, and music moguls, and they all got such a kick out of Andrei's antics.

He was *The Ice Man*, and remained in character 24-7.

As the private elevator opened to Andrei's Penthouse, which occupied the entire top floor of the building, I walked into his foyer that consisted solely of items made of chrome, glass, and white marble. It looked like he had commissioned Philippe Starck to design it.

Every door was made of smoked glass with a thick chrome frame, and opened and closed automatically, triggered by motion sensors.

As I came within five feet of each door, they slid open automatically, disappearing into the wall like a spy's high security headquarters. His walls were covered in white ostrich leather, while chrome sconces provided a glowing ambient light.

His floors were covered in white Italian marble – *Bianco Carrara Statuario* – a special marble handpicked in Milan by Andrei.

Every element of Andrei's home was designed by Andrei himself. He had very specific taste, and had a very specific eye that only chose *Andreiesque* pieces.

Unlike the rustic feel of The Icon's home and Joseph's home, Andrei's home was as modern as modern gets.

There was so much glass in his home you would have thought he was responsible for 80% of the *Windex* consumption in New York City.

His living room was massive and had white leather *Roche Bobois* sectional sofas pointing in the direction of a long, low-profile fireplace that had a thick chrome frame, matching the frames of his smoked glass doors.

Above it on the wall hung a large modern painting by a famous Cuban artist that Andrei had invited to the party, and at the click of a button, a giant 100-inch flat screen television came descending right out of the ceiling, covering the painting.

The lighting, the fireplace, and the TV were all controlled by a high-tech remote control that looked like you had to have a Master's Degree in Computer Science to operate it.

Under the $40,000 worth of *Roche Bobois* sofas was a giant white shag area rug that I'm sure many a supermodel had rolled around in with Andrei.

His dining room consisted of a giant 12-foot glass dining table, white leather and chrome chairs, and a massive white *Baccarat* crystal chandelier hanging from the mirrored ceiling.

Every room had a glass, chrome and white leather theme, except his bedroom, which had the exact same design elements as the rest of his penthouse, but in all-black gloss.

His ornate black lacquered bedframe sat below a massive black *Baccarat* chandelier, a clone of the one in his dining room, but in black gloss instead of white. Every light in his bedroom was on a dimmer, and Andrei kept every bedroom light as dim as possible.

His bedroom looked like a hotel suite for vampire billionaires.

Huge glass and chrome doors – all operated by a remote control of course – slid open from his bedroom onto a balcony that included an infinity Jacuzzi that could seat ten… just enough room for Andrei and nine supermodels.

This was the ultimate bachelor pad.

Everything about Andrei was over-the-top, including his business. He was a diamond broker and luxury jewelry designer, and was a walking advertisement for his brand.

His rings, his bracelets and his cufflinks were all custom made pieces designed by Andrei himself. His brand delivered a product so *bling'd-out* that it even made rap stars blush.

He had more luxury watches than anyone I'd ever seen. His favorite – a limited edition *Roger Dubuis* – was one of only eight made in the world, and retailed for over $300,000.

This was the only piece of jewelry he wore that wasn't his own brand. Everything else was *Andrei Ice*.

Andrei was *The Ice Man*, but by his own admission, without The Icon's financial backing back when he was getting started, Andrei would never have made it as a businessman.

The Icon had not only provided the financial backing required to get Andrei's jewelry business going. He also taught him the fundamentals of business, and eventually, how to run a company.

Andrei told me, "My father in Romania invested in me to *get* me to America. The Icon invested in me to *keep* me here. Without either of them, I don't know where the f*** I'd be now, bro. Seriously. No one would have mentored me the way The Icon did. No one would have spent that much time with me. You think I'm crazy now? You should have seen me back when The Icon first met me. I was on some crazy sh**, man. But he never tried to change me, bro. He always let me be me."

It was obvious that beneath Andrei's over-the-top bravado and rough exterior, he was an appreciative son… a dedicated protégé… and a loyal friend.

He made things fun for me in New York, and though his persona and his lifestyle was very different than Joseph's, Andrei added a much needed dimension to my journey, and was a great friend to me in the process.

It was nice having a great wingman, especially because I didn't have a co-pilot yet.

I had spent three years in New York, which seemed to go by faster than the blink of an eye. I continued to hang out with Andrei, but no more late nights.

I was putting in even more time at the firm, building it with Joseph's help. He would fly out about once a month to help me grow the firm, which I appreciated immensely.

Andrei did a lot of business at night in the clubs, promoting his jewelry company, whereas my business didn't lend itself to networking in the party scene as much. Andrei would give me a hard time about not going out more, but I knew he was just giving me a hard time. He understood my business, and respected the fact that I was so committed to The Icon.

Andrei knew my loyalty to The Icon matched his own commitment to our mentor, and for Andrei, this unsurpassed level of loyalty was what he respected and honored most.

I learned a lot from Andrei.

He taught me how to operate with swagger. He actually broke down the physiology of walking, talking and operating with bulletproof confidence. I must admit, it was kind of fun to learn this from Andrei because he'd teach me how to do it with the ladies, and then break down how to do it in business too.

There were so many similarities in the communication process between the dating world and the world of business. It was like getting a Master's Degree in Psychology from the *University of Andrei*, and I could tell that he kind of enjoyed teaching me all of these communication techniques.

The Icon didn't come out to New York much, as his travel schedule had subsided significantly. I assumed he was grooming Joseph to take on more responsibility, just as Joseph was grooming me to take on more responsibility.

I would talk to The Icon a couple of times a week, and even then, the mere sound of his voice made me feel stronger. He was the father figure I never had, and similar to Andrei, Joseph and Francisco, I owed him my life.

I had moved into an insane, high-floor apartment in *The Trump Tower*. I purchased it for $3.75 million, and it had a gorgeous view. Everything in my life was coming together... everything, with the exception of my love life.

But one Sunday morning, I woke up feeling slightly different than usual.

The air was a little bit crisper.

My vision was a little bit clearer.

I had a little more pep in my step.

I didn't think anything of it, but I felt like I was more *on* than usual. I decided to take a walk through Times Square and grab a cup of coffee. As I took my morning stroll, I called The Icon from my cell phone, just to catch up.

"Vincent, my boy! How are things?" The Icon inquired.

"Things couldn't be better, sir. Well, maybe they could. Don't get me wrong, I've never been happier. But there's one thing that's missing. I want an Isabella," I said without consciously being aware of how that sounded.

"Oh, I mean... I didn't mean it like that," I apologized.

The Icon broke out in laughter. "It's okay, Vincent. I know what you mean," he said.

"One day, it'll happen for you. You just keep focusing on building yourself. *Rule Number Fifteen: Don't focus on trying to FIND the right person. Just focus on BEING the right person, and the right person shall be revealed to you.*"

The Icon had a way of making the mysteries of life seem so simple. This set of rules continued to gradually be revealed to me.

I knew Joseph and Andrei had been taught all of the rules, and I was tempted to ask them to teach me all of them at once.

But I also knew The Icon had a system of how he would chronologically reveal them to me, and so I trusted in that, despite my insatiable curiosity.

"So, whatcha up to this morning?" The Icon inquired.

"I'm going to grab an Americano at *Madre's*," I replied.

"*Madre's*? The place we first met in LA?" he asked.

"Yeah, there's one here in Times Square," I confirmed.

"Cool. I love that place. They've really grown over the last few years. They've got stores in every major city now. Anyway, gotta run. I'm off to my yoga class. I'm into this *Bikram Yoga* thing now. They heat the room up to 115 degrees, and I sweat my butt off for 75 minutes. Great for the pores," he said.

"Okay, sir. Enjoy your class. Oh, and sir..."

I paused for a moment, smiling internally and externally as I allowed myself the luxury of soaking in what my life was becoming.

"Thank you... for... for everything."

"You're welcome, son," he graciously replied.

I could practically hear The Icon's smile through the phone. He knew how much I appreciated everything he had done for me. I always made a concerted effort to let him know the depth and magnitude of my gratitude.

As I entered *Madre's*, it dawned on me that just a few short years ago, I had a failing business, and was working out of the *Madre's* in LA every weekend.

What a trip.

I think that's why I enjoyed having a nice hot cup of coffee there. I loved *Madre's* coffee, however the real reason I liked going there was that it reminded me of the day I met The Icon – the day that would eventually change the course of my life, forever.

It allowed me to take a few moments to reminisce about *The Good Ole Days*.

I ordered my usual.

Grande Americano.

Three Splendas.

A dash of cream… and an extra shot of Espresso.

Yes, The Icon had granted me permission to be part of his *Extra Shot Of Espresso Club*. Andrei still gave me a hard time about it whenever I ordered one, but it was all in good fun.

As I sat in my normal spot, enjoying my perfectly steeped Americano, in walked an absolutely breathtaking woman wearing a high-powered *Tom Ford* skirt suit, a pair of 5-inch *Louboutin* stilettos, carrying a large black *Prada* bag.

Her hair was slicked back in a sleek ponytail, and her olive complexion was that of an Egyptian goddess. She practically floated across the floor, making me feel like I was sitting in the front row of a one-woman runway show.

As she removed her oversized *Chanel* sunglasses, my jaw hit the ground.

It was Valentina.

Chapter Fourteen
Destiny

My mind started racing.

Would she remember me?

It had been years since I first met her back in LA.

My heart stopped.

I immediately and frantically zeroed in on the ring finger of her left hand.

No rock and no ring.

I was amazed, relieved and anxious.

I would have thought some lucky billionaire had already married her.

I thought to myself, "This is destiny." After all of these years believing that my dream girl had vanished, here I was, getting my second chance.

But this version of Valentina was different. She had traded in her *Madre's* uniform for *Tom Ford* suit, and upgraded from a $30 *Nike* backpack to a $3,200 *Prada* handbag.

This, I realized, was *Valentina Version 2.0*, and I must say, it was slightly intimidating.

I scoured every inch of her body. She wore a large men's size, solid gold *Cartier Roadster* watch on her left wrist and a giant canary yellow diamond ring on the middle finger of her right hand, set in yellow gold. Simple, clean and elegant.

She had large, dark, midnight brown eyes with long, captivating lashes that practically created a tropical breeze every time she blinked. She had high cheekbones, and very full – very sexy – pouty lips.

With her hair up in a ponytail, I could see the slender nape of her neck as she turned her head from side to side. Everything she did – every move she made – looked like it was in slow motion… effortless, sultry, and perfect.

I knew I had to do something creative – something unique – to make a world-class second impression, and if she didn't remember me from our first encounter eight years ago, I would be creating a first impression.

It was game time, and the pressure was on.

I watched her out of the corner of my eye, nervously formulating my approach.

As her order came up, the barista placed her coffee on the counter top. I quickly, yet smoothly, slid in front of her, grabbing her coffee, as I pretended to start drinking it.

She stopped me saying, "Hey, I think that's my coffee."

I stopped, looked at her, and erupted in laughter.

Valentina was shocked, but began laughing with me. She had a great sense of humor, and had quickly figured out that I was just messing with her. She had a mischievously sexy grin that absolutely took my breath away.

I was very confident with the ladies at this point in my life, even a little cocky, perhaps.

But Valentina gave me butterflies in my stomach.

I had obsessed about her ever since I first met her at *Madre's* in Los Angeles, and this was my second chance to make an impression.

"Valentina, right?" I said in my most relaxed and confident voice.

"Yes... How do we... Wait a minute! *Madre's* in LA! I gave you a breakfast sandwich," she said. "That was YEARS ago! You remember me from that long ago?"

"Hey, you know they say the way to a man's heart is through his stomach! That breakfast sandwich was delicioso!" I said, trying to impress her with my broken Español.

"Oh, veo qué hablas Español!" Valentina exclaimed.

"Un poco," I said, smiling.

Valentina sat down at my table, and we talked... and talked... and talked... for over two hours. It was as comfortable as catching up with an old friend.

No games.

No posturing.

Andrei would have probably disapproved of how available I was, but I didn't care. This seemed, well, natural.

"Nice suit," Valentina commented.

"Ah, te gusta?" I flirtatiously asked, fishing for another compliment.

Thank God she dropped our little Spanish interaction after that, because that was the extent of *mi Español* abilities.

I was wearing a charcoal grey, herringbone suit and a crisp white shirt with a hand stitched Italian spread collar, unbuttoned, with no tie, tailored by Massimo, of course.

At this point in my life, my entire wardrobe was dialed in, both my business wardrobe as well as my social wardrobe.

Practically everything I wore was from The Icon's custom clothing company, tailored by Massimo himself.

My social attire usually consisted of a tailored two-buttoned suit with a wide peak lapel, an open-collared shirt, and Italian loafers... very *expensive* Italian loafers.

I now embodied The Icon's image, as did all the advisors at the firm. This was part of our culture.

Everyone, and I mean *everyone*, dressed to the nines, 24-7.

Valentina's comment had reinforced what The Icon had taught me years ago. When you're dressed like a successful, sophisticated businessman, you attract a higher caliber woman.

Image, though not everything, was important.

"So what are you doing out here in New York?" I inquired to Valentina.

"Well when I first met you, I was just getting ready to expand my business out here to the East Coast. I actually left the day after I met you," she explained.

"So what kind of business are you in?" I asked.

Valentina responded, "You're looking at it. I'm in the coffee business."

"So what do you do in the coffee business?" I asked.

"Well, I'm involved in both the wholesale and the retail side. All of our coffee comes out of South America," she said.

As we talked, I realized just how different this conversation would have gone had I never met The Icon. My career had taken quantum leaps over the last few years, and I was making more in a month than most doctors make in a year.

I had become a totally different person than I was when I first laid eyes upon Valentina back in LA eight years ago.

I was confident.

I believed in myself.

"So what's the name of the company you work for?" I asked.

"My company is called *Madre's Coffee*," she said.

"Oh, you mean *this* company... the coffee we're drinking right now. So are you in sales... or marketing... or?" I asked.

"I actually own the company," she said.

"Wow! Congratulations! I had no idea. That's amazing," I apologetically said.

She had the most unbelievable giggle.

Everything about Valentina was magnetic.

Easy to talk to.

Great sense of humor.

Not afraid to laugh at herself.

And certainly, not afraid to laugh at me.

Madre's Coffee was an emerging empire in the coffee world, a new up-and-coming brand that had gained a national presence.

"Vincent, when I met you, I was working at my first store, training my store manager to take over most of the responsibilities. This store we're in now... this is my second store," she humbly explained.

"So how many stores do you have now?" I inquired.

"Thirty-seven," she nonchalantly said, downplaying her success.

"Wow! That's awesome! Your coffee is great, by the way," I affirmed, congratulating her on her success.

I thought to myself, *"I think I just met my future wife."*

Not only was she gorgeous, but she was also charming, intelligent, and a successful entrepreneur. I remember The Icon telling me that if I was ever going to be happy, that I needed to know exactly what I wanted in a wife.

As my business grew, I had obviously faced many challenges along the way, and the lessons I learned as a result of these challenges built my character.

It made me stronger.

Talking with Valentina about her rise to success made me realize that I needed someone that had traveled the path of a struggling entrepreneur, struggling the way I had struggled.

I needed someone that understood *my* path.

But Valentina didn't just conceptually *understand* my path.

She *lived* it.

Valentina shared with me the many challenges she faced importing her coffee from South America, facing quality control issues, production issues, as well as personnel issues running the business.

She even shared her crazy experiences going deep into the jungle to meet with the coffee bean growers, and how she would have to hike several miles to get to the areas where even *H1 Hummers* could not reach.

"Vincent, I remember there was this *South American* legend about a rare coffee bean only found deep in the jungles of Peru. I had to hike into areas that only indigenous people knew about – areas that only an obsessive coffee extremist would think of venturing into. I had to negotiate with a Chief of an indigenous tribe to take me in a canoe down a parasite-infested river in search of the place where this coffee bean grows. It was so humid, sitting in a sauna would have been refreshing, comparatively. I wanted to jump in the river to cool off so badly, but I was told that if I did, the parasites in the water would literally enter through my ears and nose, lay their eggs, and when they hatched, the larva would eat my brain and I'd die a miserable death."

I found Valentina and her stories absolutely fascinating.

On the surface, she looked like a cross between a runway model and a high-powered businesswoman, yet she obviously wasn't afraid to roll up her sleeves and get dirty.

This was a woman after my own heart.

We began dating for several months, and the more I got to know her, the more our bond grew.

I was falling in love.

It wasn't the kind of infatuation that most lust-based relationships are built on. Though trust me when I say this… I did lust after her constantly.

But the core of our relationship was based on a mutual respect and admiration for one another.

It was the first relationship I'd ever had where I felt truly appreciated. She truly respected me and what I had gone through to achieve the level of success that I had achieved.

Valentina also knew what to say when I was stressed out about business, because she understood first-hand what I was going through as an entrepreneur.

She never complained about my long hours, partially because she worked just as hard as I did, perhaps even harder.

190

Indirectly, her work ethic actually pushed me to work harder, shifting me into higher gears that I didn't even know existed within myself.

We talked about every aspect of our lives, except for one area. Valentina didn't talk much about her parents.

Perhaps she sensed that I wasn't too fond of talking about *my* parents. But she did seem to have a close relationship with them however.

Apparently, she came from a relatively wealthy family because she shared with me that when she started her coffee business, her family offered to give her the seed money to get it off the ground. But Valentina respectfully turned it down.

She wanted to do it on her own.

When her parents found out how much the banks were charging her in interest, they even offered to give her a lower interest loan, but she still declined, wanting to build everything with no special advantages.

One night at dinner, Valentina told me, "Vincent, I know you understand this, but I'm going to tell you anyway. Pain is temporary, but pride is forever. Remember the pain you went through in the beginning of your career, back when you had to eat Top Ramen and oatmeal for dinner? Remember when you used to worry about whether or not you were going to have rent money at the end of each month? Well, that pain was temporary... but pride is forever."

She continued, "When you overcome adversities the way you have – the way my parents have – the pride you carry inside is invaluable. You see, I grew up with money, and I'm proud of my parents for what they accomplished... but I wanted that feeling of pride that they had. They did it all on their own, and so I wanted to model my career after theirs."

It was this kind of wisdom that I grew to love in Valentina.

She *got it*.

Just as Isabella *got it*, so did Valentina.

I often thought about Isabella and the confidence she instilled in me during the many dinners at The Icon's home.

I remember how she came rushing to my defense when Joseph's wife questioned *The New Girlfriend Talk*.

And I remember what she told me about what I was worth, and how I shouldn't settle. If Isabella were to ever meet my Valentina, I think she would be proud of me.

I had spent the last eight years investing in myself, focusing on bettering myself. And just as *Rule Number Fifteen* had promised, as soon as I stopped trying to *find* the right person, and I just focused on *being* the right person, Valentina magically appeared.

The wisdom of the rules never stopped amazing me.

As we finished our dinner, I briefly excused myself from the table to use the restroom, and as I walked into the men's room, I briefly caught my reflection in the mirror. The sharply dressed, successful businessman I saw looking back at me in the mirror had come a long way from being the struggling wanna-be entrepreneur I had once been. And in that moment, it dawned on me that I had finally become the man I so desperately wanted to be.

For the first time in my life, I was proud of myself. Not too many people can look in the mirror and honestly say that.

I thought back to the first conversation I'd ever had with Andrei, when he told me that the greatest pleasure in life is accomplishing things that other people said you could not do.

And there I was, a successful businessman, dating the woman of my dreams. And I had business mentors whom I respected tremendously, that respected me too.

It had been such a long time coming, but in retrospect, it made me appreciate *The Good Ole Days* even more... the days back when I was broke.

When I returned to the table, Valentina informed me that she had taken the liberty of ordering desert for us.

"Cool! What'd you get us?" I inquired.

"Pecan pie. I hope that's okay with you," she said.

My heart soared as my spirit smiled inside.

"It's perfect," I said, with a nostalgic grin.

I believe there are subtle moments in life where God reminds you that He has a sense of humor, where He sends you little messages using private inside jokes between you and Him.

This was one of those moments.

And in this moment, He was sending me a very special message... a message that was a defining moment in my life... an acknowledgement of all of my hard work.

It was a confirmation that my sacrifices were not in vain... that my suffering was worth it.

It was as if God was whispering in my ear saying, *"Whatsoever a man soweth, that shall he reap... and Vincent, it's your turn to reap now."*

Chapter Fifteen
The Valentina Effect

Valentina gave me an entirely different perspective on success. She came from a wealthy family, but was determined to achieve success on her own merit.

This was a quality in Valentina that affected me like an aphrodisiac. To me, there was nothing sexier than a successful woman that did it on her own.

She rarely talked about her parents, but from what I gathered, they had money – *serious money*.

But despite her family's wealth, Valentina was dead set on proving that she could succeed on her own, without their help.

The only advantage that she had regarding her parents' resources was that they paid for her education.

She had gone to The Wharton School of Business, and that kind of educational pedigree was impressive in any business environment.

Valentina told me, "It was important to my mother that I go to college and study business. Even as a little girl, she would tell me, *'Valentina, education is something that no one can ever take away from you... and as a woman, it's important to be in a position where no one can question how you got to the top,'* which I understood. Perhaps I overcompensated in this area, but I wanted to be able to walk into a room of successful businessmen and make it impossible for them to refute the legitimacy of my success."

I had never thought about success from a female perspective. Valentina was stunning, and when I thought about it, I could see how people might be jealous of her success and attempt to discredit her accomplishments.

They might attempt to accuse her of using her beauty to get by, or perhaps her family's wealth and connections to set the table for her.

But Valentina had masterfully orchestrated the architecture of her life to make it impossible to find anything to refute her success.

She had an educational background that you couldn't argue with. She had the intelligence and communication skills that you couldn't deny. And she had the work ethic and tenacity that made most businessmen look like little boys.

From a business perspective, she transcended gender, beauty and ethnicity. She was, regardless of any of these elements, a heavy hitter.

When I first met her in that brief interaction at *Madre's* eight years ago back in Los Angeles, she had just gotten her first coffee house established. She told me that store was the *test pilot store*. It had taken her two years to build that location to the point where it could run on autopilot.

Valentina told me, "The first location is always the hardest. Sure, you've got the basics of the business that have to be solidified, like developing a consistently brilliant product, hiring and training good personnel, executing good marketing, finding a good location... the list goes on. You've got cash flow analysis... loan interest decisions... commercial real estate negotiations... cross-branding opportunities. But in addition to these basics, you've got to build and solidify a system-driven business."

Our conversations weren't like any conversations I'd experienced before with girlfriends.

They had substance, real substance.

With other girls I'd gone out with, the only real thing they had going for them was their looks. Beyond that, they were hollow inside.

They were *Drop Dead Stupid*.

But Valentina wasn't just drop dead gorgeous and incredibly intelligent. She had a breadth of world experiences that would impress any entrepreneur.

Valentina continued, "The first thing I had to do after I got my first location up and running successfully, was figure out what processes I could duplicate, from an operations standpoint. Operationally, things worked at my first location because I touched every process. I was 100% hands-on. I was a total control freak."

"But isn't that what makes someone successful in business? I'm a self-admitted control freak too. That's what made me successful, and that's probably what made you successful too," I said.

"Initially, yes. But you can only go so far when your business is 100% reliant on you. You've got to develop systems – systems that you can duplicate in every location's operations. The biggest lesson I learned from my first location was that if I were to expand into multiple locations, I would have to develop a system-driven business. I would have to develop a business that didn't rely on me having to babysit every little detail. Trust me, for a control freak like me, that was not an easy thing to do," Valentina explained.

Valentina wasn't just a gun-slinging entrepreneur.

She was a bona fide businesswoman.

Sure, I was successful too. But my success came from working hard under The Icon's system. Not to take anything away from my success. I did work awfully hard. But Valentina developed her own systems, from nothing.

"I continued to handle everything from a branding and marketing standpoint, as well as product development. I mean, I still go down to South America twice a year to meet with my coffee growers. But from a systems standpoint, after I developed my operations protocol and trained my staff, I had to trust in my system and step away. I realized that in order to expand to the level I had envisioned, that I would have to relinquish control of the day-to-day operations, and let my system run the day-to-day, as I focused on expanding the brand," she said.

As I listened to Valentina talk about her experiences, I became more and more impressed.

"So once you got your system down, is that when you opened your second location in New York City?" I asked.

She responded, "Exactly. But my system continues to evolve. The better you get, the better you better get. I believe that if you're not progressing, no matter how successful you are, then you're falling behind. There's no such thing as being static. The rest of the world is moving ahead, and so if you're not progressing at a pace that out-paces the rest of the world, then you're getting passed by, left behind in the dust. There's no such thing as being the *same as yesterday.* You're either getting better, or you're getting worse."

The discipline Valentina had was maniacal.

When it came to business, she was a machine.

"My New York store presented different challenges than my LA store did, however the core system still applied. I had to get my employees 100% on board, believing in the principles of my system. Once I accomplished this, the system was running the business, and I could move on and open another location. Someday, I'll open locations overseas, but for now, I'm looking at developing a new summer drink. I think it's going to be a big hit," Valentina calculated.

The concept of having a system this delineated reminded me of how Francisco taught me how to present a hotel guest with a chilled bottle of water.

Then all of a sudden, it hit me.

The successful, polished businesswoman that sat in front of me was the same girl I met in the Los Angeles *Madre's* eight years ago.

I was now 34-years old.

When we had first met, I was only twenty-six. I had grown so much in these eight years, both as a businessman and as a man. But Valentina had also gone through tremendous growth as well. In eight years, she had built a coffee empire from just one store to thirty-seven stores.

I asked her, "If you don't mind me asking you, how old were you when we first met?"

"I was 27-years old. I finished my MBA program at Wharton when I was twenty-three, and I opened my first *Madre's* location – the one in LA – when I was twenty-five. It took me almost two years to get it to the point where I felt comfortable opening up store number two," she said.

Valentina was an old soul, and had accomplished so much in her life. To think that the girl who gave me a free breakfast sandwich eight years ago – who I thought was just a coffee shop barista – actually owned the place, and would go on to open thirty-seven locations, building an empire all on her own.

I did the math in my head, and realized that Valentina was 35-years old, just one year older than me. She looked like she was twenty-five, but had the sophistication of a woman well beyond her years.

I wondered about her past relationships, and why she hadn't gotten married in her twenties. After about six months of us seriously dating, I asked her.

She said, "I had a few boyfriends along the way. Most of them couldn't handle my success or my commitment to my business. Those boyfriends washed out pretty quickly. But I did have one serious boyfriend for just under a year. He was a very successful businessman."

"So how'd you meet him?" I inquired.

"I met him on a blind date. In fact, my father actually set us up. He was a good guy, but he wasn't in the frame of mind to settle down, and quite frankly, neither was I. We were both heavily pursuing our careers, and there just wasn't enough time in the day to build our empires and have a serious relationship at the same time," Valentina explained.

Hearing this made me realize just how important *timing* is in life. So many things have to line up properly, from a timing perspective, to make things work.

If Valentina and I had started dating back when I first met her, I wouldn't have been ready. I wouldn't have been deserving of such a high caliber woman because I was a mess back then. Neither my career, nor my confidence, had been developed yet.

Plus, I wouldn't have had *time* for a relationship.

I was in the very first stages of establishing my career and my relationship with The Icon. I was interning 12-hours a day at the firm, and then working my night shift at *The Hotel 100*, plus my weekend shifts too.

In addition, during that time, Valentina was in the midst of building her coffee empire, moving to New York, developing her brand and traveling all over the world.

We were reunited at the perfect time.

My business was booming, and her business was booming too. We had both struggled through the beginning stages of our careers, and had both come out on top.

I thought for a moment that it might have been cool for us to struggle together, and build our empires as a couple. But the more I thought about it, I'm glad we built our businesses separately.

I think it's important for a couple to have their own identities and their own successes, independent of each other.

Valentina and I had lived parallel lives for the last eight years – her on the East Coast, and me on the West Coast. We had started at the bottom, and now we were on top of the world.

I asked her, "So that was the only serious relationship you ever had?"

"Well, there was another one that lasted about a year. It was during my last year at Wharton. He was an ex-runway model-turned-actor who had done a few movies and his career looked like it was about to take off. He would want me to go to these movie premiers and Hollywood industry events with him all the time, but I couldn't go. I was finishing up my MBA," she said.

"When I finished, I moved back to LA to open my first coffee house, and he thought I would spend more time with him, but I was working sixteen to eighteen hour days. When my days were over, I just wanted to go home and prepare for the next day," Valentina explained.

"So let me guess. He couldn't take the fact that you were more committed to your business than to him?" I guessed.

Valentina responded, "Well, let's just say that I wasn't going to let anyone or anything stand in the way of me building my empire. He obviously wasn't on board with the program."

"So he felt threatened by your independence?" I inquired.

Valentina smiled, and softly giggled to herself.

I knew that meant I was right.

"When I broke up with him, he was so mad at me. I think I kind of crushed his ego. He told me *'Go ahead with your stupid coffee business. You're never gonna make it. You'll be working at Starbucks in a year.'* That just fueled my fire," Valentina said.

She went on to tell me that the *Starbucks* comment her ex-boyfriend made drove her to be even more successful.

"When he said those things to me, I made a commitment to myself that I would never let a man talk to me like that again. I also made a commitment to build my empire to the level where every time he saw the *Madre's* brand – whether it was one of my coffee houses, or my brand being served in a luxury resort, or my coffee beans being sold at a grocery store – that he'd be reminded of his words of stupidity," Valentina said.

It was kind of endearing seeing this beautiful, statuesque, businesswoman outwardly dog an ex-boyfriend.

She was classy, but had a certain quality about her that let you know that she was tough as nails – driven and relentless in her pursuit of building her empire.

"Vincent, you want to know what my greatest motivator is?" Valentina asked.

"What?" I inquired.

"Revenge. Not in a *vengeful* sort of way, but in a way that makes all the people that ever bet against you feel sick to their stomachs when they see your success, because they have to eat their words," Valentina articulated.

"So what's this ex-boyfriend doing now? Is he still an actor?" I inquired.

"Sort of. He's still trying to make it big, but he hasn't gotten much work ever since we broke up," she said.

"Wait a minute. That was over eleven years ago. How does he pay his bills if he hasn't booked many acting gigs in the last eleven years?" I asked.

"The last I heard, he had a part-time job to pay the bills while he continues to try to get his acting career off the ground," Valentina admitted.

"Doing what?" I asked.

Valentina cracked a devilish grin and said, "He's a barista at Starbucks."

Chapter Sixteen
The Revelation

Another year had flown by.

Valentina and I were inseparable.

I told Andrei I was seeing someone, but I never gave him any details about her, and I never let them meet. In fact, I never even told him her name. There are some things, I believe, that are meant to be kept private.

Surprisingly, Andrei never gave me a hard time about *being in love*. In fact, it was just the opposite.

He was actually happy for me.

Andrei got a kick out of taking me out partying back when I first arrived in New York, but I think he knew that the club scene wasn't *my scene*.

He and I grew to be very close friends.

We talked on the phone at least once a month. I'll always be grateful towards Andrei for taking me under his wing, getting me acclimated to New York City.

I would also keep Valentina away from Joseph when he came to town. Andrei, Joseph, and The Icon were like family to me, and I didn't want to introduce Valentina to them until I was sure she was the one.

But after a year, I knew.

Valentina was the one, no doubt about it.

Her coffee business continued to grow, and my firm was knocking the cover off the ball. We were the ultimate young power couple.

I finally mustered up the guts to tell The Icon about my relationship with Valentina. I gushed about her on the phone to him, and he was so happy for me.

"So what's the lucky gal's name?" The Icon asked.

"Valentina," I replied.

"Valentina? Wow, that's a beautiful name. So how'd you two meet?" he inquired.

"You're not going to believe this, sir. I met her about nine years ago at *Madre's Coffee House* in LA where I met you... and as fate would have it, I ran into her at the *Madre's* out here in New York. Can you believe that? And that's not it. She actually owns the company. She owns *Madre's Coffee*! She's an entrepreneur, just like me!" I exclaimed.

"Wow! That's amazing. That sounds like destiny!" he said. Then he paused for a moment, and asked, "Are you treating her right?"

"Of course, sir," I replied, laughing his question off a bit.

"Vincent, I'm serious. When you meet that special someone, where you have a bond like Isabella and I have... like Joseph and Christine have... you treat her like gold. You've got to protect that relationship with your life. *Rule Number Sixteen: Once you get married, it's you and your spouse against the world,*" The Icon told me.

I remembered the inscription inside Isabella's *Rolex* that she shared with me that read, '*Us Against The World.*'

That was their bond – The Icon's commitment to Isabella, and Isabella's commitment to The Icon. That was what I wanted with Valentina, and I felt she wanted the same.

"There's only one thing," I told The Icon. "She doesn't talk much about her family... where they're from... what they do. Nothing. Is that something I should be worried about?"

"Hey, look at me. I don't talk much about my family, especially my father. You don't talk much about yours either. Neither does Isabella. Maybe she's the same," The Icon reassured me.

"Maybe you're right," I said, feeling better about the situation. "Sir, I'd really love for you and Isabella to meet her. I've got a trip planned to come out to LA at the end of the month to meet with Joseph regarding some new financial portfolios. Would it be okay if I brought her so you all could meet?"

"Vincent, that sounds like a great plan. Isabella and I would love to meet her. I'm sure Joseph will be happy as well. Does he know about her?" The Icon asked.

"He knows *of* her, but I haven't told him any details," I said.

"Well, there you have it. She hasn't told you much about her family, and you haven't told me and Joseph much about her!" he said, slightly giving me a hard time.

I guess he had a point.

We had planned the trip, but it still bothered me a bit. That evening, over dinner, I confronted Valentina about it.

"Can I ask you a question? It's kind of personal," I said.

"Of course, honey," she replied.

"How come you never talk about your family?" I asked.

"Vincent, the truth is, I'm a very private person. In fact, I've never taken a boyfriend home to meet my folks, excluding the guy my father set me up with. I guess I kind of feel that it's got to be the right guy," she said.

"Valentina, you're everything I've ever wanted in a woman. You're the one I want to spend the rest of my life with, and I'm ready to take that next step with you," I said. "But I'm old fashioned. I want to ask you to marry me, and…"

She cut me off, jumping into my arms, kissing me passionately. By her response, I knew she felt the same.

Then she said, "Vincent, I've known you were the one ever since…"

"Okay, okay, but wait," I interjected. "I'm old fashioned. I want to ask you to marry me, but out of respect, I feel it's only right for me to ask your father's permission first. I'm going to LA on business to meet with one of my partners, and I want you to come with me to meet three very special people. My mentor, his wife, and dear friend of mine. Will you come with me?"

"I'd love to meet them!" she exclaimed.

"Now, I also know your folks live somewhere in LA, and I really want to meet them too. I want to ask for your father's permission, that is, assuming you want to marry me too," I said.

"You KNOW I want to marry you. Isn't it obvious?" she exclaimed again.

"So can I meet your folks?" I asked again.

Valentina paused. Then she smiled, held me close, and said, "I would love for you to meet my parents. They're going to love you... everything about you."

"So you never answered my original question. Why don't you ever talk about them?" I asked.

"Vincent, I'm VERY close to my parents. Every night, after I hang up the phone with you, I call them. My father... he's a wonderful man. He set the bar for me when it came to dating guys. That's why I never took any of my boyfriends home to meet him. None of them were worthy," Valentina said.

Then she put her arms around me, looking deep into my eyes and said, "But you... Vincent, my dad is going to love you. And my mom, she taught me to be a strong, independent woman. The main reason I'm so driven is that I've always wanted to make my mom proud of the woman I've become. I've always wanted to make both of my parents proud. That's why I never took any of my boyfriends home to meet them. None of them measured up."

Valentina was a wise, calculated woman that operated by strong principles and beliefs.

She continued, "That's also why I never wanted to accept their help, financially. I wanted to prove to them, and to myself, that I could do it on my own."

"And you did!" I said.

Valentina smiled, and in a soft, modest voice, she confirmed, "And I did."

"But you still didn't answer the question about why you never talk about them. What's the reason?" I asked again.

"Vincent, my parents are very wealthy. Not just *kind of* wealthy. They're *extremely* wealthy. Like I told you before, I'm incredibly proud of what they've accomplished. I am. But I also know that sometimes, when people find out that you come from a family of wealth, they don't acknowledge your success. They assume that your success is due to your family's influence, or your family's resources. I never wanted people to think of me like that," she explained.

"But I'm not like that. It's obvious to me that you built your business all on your own, based on your own merit. Within five minutes of hearing you talk about your business, I could tell you built it from the ground up. It's obvious," I said.

"That's why I love you. And that's why I'm going to introduce you to my parents. And that's why I'm going to marry you!" she said, beaming ear to ear.

I orchestrated a dinner with The Icon and Isabella, Joseph and Christine, Francisco and his brothers and sister, and as luck would have it, Andrei was planning on being in LA that week, so I invited him too.

I made reservations at *Amor*, the hottest Latin-fusion celebrity-frequented restaurant in Beverly Hills, not far from *The Hotel 100*.

It would be a celebration.

I would announce to those closest to me that Valentina and I were to be engaged.

The next two weeks flew by, and on the plane ride from JFK to LAX, I reflected on how much my life had changed.

I was making more in a week than I used to make in a year. I was running the hottest boutique wealth management firm in New York City. I was getting engaged to the woman of my dreams. I had friends – mentors – that I could trust like big brothers.

I was blessed.

I told Valentina that we'd be staying at *The Hotel 100*.

"It's an amazing hotel in Beverly Hills. Have you ever heard of it?" I asked, hoping to impress her.

"Of course. My parents and I used to go there all the time," she said, as if it were an everyday thing for her.

I guess her parents were pretty darn wealthy if they frequented *The Hotel 100* on a regular basis.

As we walked in the main entrance, a young kid with a million dollar smile enthusiastically greeted us, saying, "Welcome back, sir. Chilled bottle of water... compliments of *The Hotel 100.*"

Francisco had obviously taught him well.

I was hoping to run into Francisco. I hadn't seen him for almost a year, and I was dying to introduce him to Valentina, but he wasn't there. Perhaps it was his day off. I figured he'd meet her at dinner anyway.

As we walked through the lobby, people couldn't help but stare at Valentina. When she walked into a room, she commanded that kind of attention.

The hotel workers stared at her like she was a celebrity, and Valentina, being the modest, gracious woman that she is, graciously smiled at them, acknowledging them as being no less important than her.

It made me proud to be with a woman with that kind of presence.

We checked into our room, unpacked and freshened up a bit, then headed off to *Amor* for dinner. I had arranged a private dining room for our party. I wanted to do something special for everyone, for they had certainly done countless special things for me.

We entered the restaurant and were immediately greeted by a very attractive, young hostess.

"You must be Vincent," she said. "Your private room is prepared for you, and your guests are awaiting your arrival. Please follow me."

With my hand gently placed on the small of her back, I escorted Valentina, guiding her down the long, dark hallway to *The Primero Room*, the private room I had reserved.

As we entered the room, there everyone was.

The Icon.

Isabella.

Joseph and Christine.

And Andrei.

The most important people in my life, all gathered together to meet my future bride.

I exclaimed, "Everyone, I'd like you to meet the love of my life, Valentina!"

"What the f***?" Andrei blurted out.

"Papa?" Valentina exclaimed as she looked at The Icon.

"Valentina?" Isabella screamed, as she ran over and smothered her with hugs and kisses.

Joseph stood there speechless.

I was totally confused.

I looked at The Icon as he stood calmly with his hands clasped together. He had the biggest smile I'd ever seen on his face.

He said, "Valentina, sweetheart. This is Vincent, my protégé. Vincent, this is my little girl – *my daughter* – Valentina."

I, along with Andrei and Joseph, stood there dumbfounded.

Isabella immediately figured out exactly what had happened, and shortly thereafter, I figured it out too.

"Sir, you mean to tell me you knew about this all along?" I exclaimed, approaching The Icon.

"Vincent, as you know, I believe in destiny. I believe in fate. When you moved to New York, I believed in my heart that you would meet my daughter. I didn't know how, but I believed," he explained.

The Icon continued, "Vincent, do you remember the first time you told me about Valentina on the phone? When you told me about her, my heart skipped a beat. And when you told me she owned *Madre's Coffee*, I obviously knew you were talking about my little girl. Fate had come into fruition."

"Bro, you gotta be f***in' kidding me!" Andrei said again in disbelief. "Bro, your fiancé is Valentina? No f***in' way man!"

Andrei came around the table, and picked me up off the ground in a bear hug. He was so ecstatic about the whole situation. It was the first time I'd ever seen Andrei get emotional like this. Even he was misty-eyed.

He said, "Bro, these ain't tears, okay. My eyeballs are just sweatin' a little bit."

Isabella chimed in placing her warm hands on my cheeks, "Vincent! I had no idea! This is the Lord's blessing. This is a mother's dream come true!"

It all made sense to me. That's why Valentina reminded me so much of Isabella. She was just like her mother.

They were both in tears… tears of joy.

Joseph came up and gave me a big hug as well. "Vincent, you're a lucky man. I've known Valentina ever since she was a schoolgirl. And look at her now! And Valentina, you have one of the finest young men I've ever met. Vincent's like a little brother to me. Congratulations to both of you."

Valentina and Isabella were still embracing, half giggling and half sobbing tears of joy.

"Papa! This whole time, you're telling me you knew? You knew Vincent and I were together?" Valentina exclaimed.

The Icon smiled, with his all-knowing smile. Though not an evangelistically religious man, he was a man of great faith.

The Icon had a real relationship with God, and had more spiritual discernment than anyone I'd ever met. He had an uncanny optimistic perspective on life, and believed in his heart of hearts, that if you lived *right* – if you lived by the *right* principles – that things would work out in the end.

It was a hard thing to dispute.

I looked at his life as the blueprint for everything I wanted to accomplish in life, and I believed that if I followed his lead, that I would one day be able to follow in his footsteps.

It happened for Andrei.

It happened for Joseph.

It even happened for Francisco.

And now it was happening for me.

Not only did I have an amazing career that was continuing to escalate... and not only did I have amazing mentors that were willing to teach me the lessons of life... but I was also about to marry the love of my life, who was the epitome of everything The Icon stood for – his very own daughter.

"Vincent, you had no idea?" Valentina said in disbelief.

"Honey, I had no idea. This entire time, your father is the man I've been telling you about. He's The Icon. He's my mentor. Everything I am in life is due to your father's mentorship. And now," I said, embracing The Icon, "With your permission, sir..."

I got choked up.

My bottom lip quivered, and I had a huge lump in my throat. My heart was pounding like Japanese *taiko* drums.

I looked The Icon in the eyes, and continued, "With your permission, sir... I would like, more than anything... to marry your daughter. May I have your blessing?"

The room erupted in cheers and applause, and without any verbal response, The Icon smiled, nodding his head in approval.

He had of course, believed all along.

I asked him, "Sir, did you know this whole time? Did you know I would one day marry Valentina?"

"No, I didn't *know*. But I *believed*," The Icon said.

Joseph exclaimed, *"Rule Number Seventeen: You don't have to know. You just have to believe!"*

The Icon said, "Knowing is based on *facts*. Believing is based on *faith*."

He didn't have to explain.

I immediately understood.

Believing was something I never struggled with. Sure, I doubted, but I believed.

I believed that meeting The Icon would change my life.

I believed that Andrei and Joseph were sincere in their intentions of taking me under their wing.

I believed that I had a shot at becoming successful by working under these incredible men.

And I believed that one day, I would cross paths with the girl I'd met at *Madre's Coffee House* way back when.

I, like The Icon, believed in fate.

I turned to Valentina, and said, "I wanted to do this in front of the people most important to me, and I had planned to do this after I received your father's blessing... which was supposed to be tomorrow night... but under the circumstances, I get to do it all at once."

I dropped down on bended knee in front of everyone and continued, "Valentina – love of my life – will you marry me?"

If you were in that restaurant at that moment, you would have thought you were sitting courtside at the NBA finals, as your favorite team hit the game winning shot at the buzzer.

Everyone went crazy.

And just as the evening couldn't get any better, Francisco and his two brothers and sister walked in.

"What's going on in here? Did someone win the lottery or something?" he asked.

"Yes," I replied. "I did."

Chapter Seventeen
Legacy

Two years had passed since that incredible evening.

Valentina and I had a small, intimate wedding ceremony, and we honeymooned on the island of Capri in Italy, as well as in Positano on the Amalfi Coast.

Business was booming, both at the firm, as well as with the expansion of *Madre's Coffee*. Everything had come together, and I didn't take any of it for granted.

Every morning, I'd wake up... sit on the edge of our bed for a moment... and thank God for blessing me with this incredible life – a life I could never have fathomed.

But one Sunday morning, I received a call from Isabella. The tone of her voice was different. She sounded extremely troubled and distraught.

"Hola, Vincent. It's Isabella. Do you have a moment to talk?" she asked.

"Of course," I said.

"Are you in a place where you can talk privately?" she asked.

"Umm... Sure, let me go out on the terrace," I said. "Is everything okay?"

"Vincent, I have to tell you something that my husband doesn't want you to know," she said in a very somber tone. "Vincent, he's sick... very sick."

"He's been battling pancreatic cancer for over five years, and he thought he could beat it. That's why he stopped eating meat, and primarily eats steamed vegetables," Isabella explained.

I remembered the first time The Icon told me he was on a new vegetable-based diet, taking all those vitamin supplements. I thought he was just on a new health kick, but in that moment, I realized the real reason. He was battling the same type of cancer that had taken my mother's life.

Never in the last five years had I heard The Icon complain about not feeling well. He looked great, like he was in top-notch shape. Little did I know the doctors had given him a 6-month death sentence five years ago.

Isabella continued, "When the doctors diagnosed him, they gave him a maximum of six months to live. But you know my husband. He's determined and takes everything head on. His cancer diagnosis was no different. He did tons of research, and worked with several holistic healers and health professionals, searching for a way to beat it. He tried Ayurvedic Medicine, herbal concoctions, and just about every naturopathic medicine possible. It's extended his life from six months to over five years. But he's starting to decline rapidly."

My heart sank.

There were several things in life that I was not good at handling, and this was one of them.

I didn't know what to say.

I just sat there, silently.

"Vincent, I've known about this all along, and my husband has made peace with it. I've made peace with it. But I'm afraid of how Valentina is going to handle it," Isabella said.

"We'll get on the first flight out tomorrow morning. Do you want to talk to her, or do you want me to break the news to her?" I asked.

"That's very sweet of you, but I'd like to be the one to tell her," Isabella confirmed.

I called Valentina out onto the terrace, handed her the phone, and excused myself. As I walked inside, I sat down on a stool in our kitchen, watching Valentina through the window onto our terrace.

I sat there watching, as she began to sob uncontrollably. I don't know if it was more painful to receive the news of my mentor's deteriorating health, or to watch Valentina receive that same news about her father.

I immediately got online and started booking our flights.

The next morning, we were on the first flight out from JFK to LAX. That was the longest 5-hour flight I'd ever been on. All Valentina and I could do was hold hands, as never-ending tears streamed down our faces.

I hadn't seen The Icon for about four months, and I didn't know what to expect. As the car service dropped us off in front of his home, we slowly walked up to the front door.

It felt like I was wearing 10-pound ankle weights.

Before we even knocked, Isabella opened the front door, immediately falling into both of our arms. It looked as though she was dehydrated, having already cried out all of her tears.

The Icon and Isabella had kept his illness a secret from everyone, including their own daughter. They kept it from Francisco. They kept it from Joseph and Andrei. And of course, they kept it from me. Imagine, keeping a secret like that from your family for over 5 years.

It angered and confused me that he hadn't shared this with us, and I wondered why.

As we walked into the living room, there he was, The Icon, sitting in his favorite leather chair, smiling.

"Hey kids! What's up?" he said as enthusiastically as he could.

The Icon had lost at least forty pounds.

The *007esque* Icon I was used to seeing looked frail, but his spirit was as strong as ever.

As we ate dinner, The Icon asked me tons of questions about how I was doing, and what my thoughts were about the development of the firm.

He asked Valentina about how the expansion of more coffee stores overseas was shaping up.

He talked about how Isabella's vegetable garden in the backyard was doing, boasting about how flavorful her heirloom tomatoes were this past season.

He talked about everything, except himself.

After dinner, Isabella and Valentina remained at the dinner table, talking about the obvious, as The Icon and I excused ourselves from the table and took a walk outside, sitting down on the chaise lounges out back, next to the pool.

I whispered, "Sir, I... I don't know what to say... I..."

"Vincent, it's okay," The Icon said, smiling, as he put his hand on my shoulder, consoling me.

"The doctors originally gave me only six months to live. That was over five years ago. I've been living on borrowed time, and the last five years have been the best five years of my life. I have an amazing family... a wife who loves me... the best son-in-law I could ask for... and my daughter is married to the man of her dreams. I'm lucky."

"Sir, forgive me for saying this, but I'm a little upset with you," I hesitantly said.

The Icon smiled. He knew what I was alluding to.

"Vincent. Son. If I had told you, it wouldn't have changed the situation. You couldn't have done anything to change the situation. I didn't want anyone to worry about me, and I really did think I was going to be able to beat this thing."

"But... but you... you didn't have to face this alone," I said, doing my very best to restrain my tears.

And there he stood.

A man who was dying of cancer, consoling *me*.

A man who knew he probably had less than a year to live, telling me that he was *lucky*.

The Icon was my hero.

He said, "Vincent, *Rule Number Eighteen: Be thankful for what you have, while you work for what you want.* Don't focus so much on what you don't have, that you lose sight of what you DO

216

have. So many people expect everything in their life to be perfect and convenient. The reality of life is that about 10% of everything in your life will get screwed up. 10% of everything you buy won't work right. 10% of every business deal you touch is doomed from the beginning. 10% of every flight you're on will be delayed. Sometimes it'll be your fault. Sometimes it'll be someone else's fault. And sometimes, it'll be no one's fault."

The Icon continued, "You've got to accept this as part of life... because what that means is that 90% of the time, you have the *opportunity* to make something happen. That doesn't mean that 90% of everything in life will be perfect. It just means that 90% of the time, you have the *opportunity* to do something great. I choose to live in that 90%. And I choose to be *grateful* for that 90%."

The Icon, even in his withered, cancer-infested state, still had the wisdom and sharpness he did when I first met him. He never stopped teaching me, and I knew that I would forever carry with me the many lessons he taught me.

He said, "Vincent, do you remember when we sat in my living room and I made the announcement regarding you launching our New York office?"

I replied, "Of course. How could I forget?"

"Well, earlier that week was when I was diagnosed with cancer. I debated on whether or not to tell everyone. I thought about whether or not it was fair to keep people in the dark... even my own family. I didn't want to rob them of knowing the truth. But I really did believe I was going to be able to lick this thing. And there was only one person I felt needed to know... to face this thing head on with me... and that was Isabella. I knew I could trust her to not tell anyone... to be my co-pilot through all of this... to fight this thing together. And I thought we would win. I came home from the doctor's office, and told her, *'Honey, we've got a new project to focus on together.'*"

"Sounds exciting!" Isabella responded, with the same enthusiastic spirit as she always had.

"Well, this one... this one's a little more serious. I just came back from the doctor, and he told me I've got this little cancer issue... but I've got a strategy on how we're going to beat it. And I'm going to need you to keep this between us. Valentina can't know. Neither can Francisco, Joseph or Andrei. And Vincent... we can't let him know about this either."

Isabella was a strong woman. Any fear or worry she ever had was overshadowed by her faith in her husband's discernment, as well her own inner strength.

She put 100% of her trust and faith in The Icon's vision, and The Icon had always valued her perspective.

In the midst of breaking the news to Isabella, The Icon said, "Honey, I believe this is the right thing to do... to fight this thing behind closed doors. I really do. But out of respect for you, I'll only withhold this from our family if you think this is the right thing too. How do you feel about this?"

Isabella scrutinized the issue, weighing the positives and negatives of either decision. And after much deliberation, they collectively decided to take on the fight together, in private, with victory as their only option.

Isabella's response to The Icon's question was simple.

"Us Against The World," she responded.

And from that moment, the fight was on.

For the next five years, Isabella made it her life's purpose to research every therapy available.

Experimental medicine.

Naturopathic therapies.

Ayurvedic medicine.

She would stay up late into the night after The Icon had gone to sleep, talking to doctors in Asia and Europe, researching every possible avenue, overturning every rock in existence.

Isabella was committed to the process like a scientist gunning to win the Nobel Peace Prize. But her prize – her husband – made any recognition-focused prize seem meaningless.

She was in the fight of her life.

"Vincent, I really believed that I could beat it, but in the event that I couldn't, I wanted to make sure that you had the opportunity to open your own firm. I've always thought of you as a son, even before you met Valentina. So I figured if I really only had six months to live, I wanted to be able to see you open your own firm," he said.

"It's not *my* firm, sir. It's *your* firm," I respectfully clarified.

"Not any more, Vincent. I had my attorneys draw up the contracts last night. The New York office is now yours, and Joseph will take ownership of the LA office. I'm just grateful I was able to live long enough to see you two men successfully run the show," The Icon said.

The Icon knew that the end was near, and though he had an inner-peace about it, he felt compelled to teach me five more *rules*.

"Vincent, I'm not just saying this because Valentina is my daughter, but this is the key to communication in your marriage, and really, communication in general... even in business. A lot of people don't really hear where the other person is coming from in a conversation. It's because they're listening to *respond*, versus listening to *understand*. The whole time the other person is talking, they're formulating what to say in response, eagerly awaiting the opportunity to jump in and respond. That's not *truly* listening. *Rule Number Nineteen: Don't listen to respond. Listen to understand*," The Icon explained.

"If you want to have a successful marriage, you've got to listen with the intention of *understanding* where your wife is coming from. Women are emotional beings, and often times, not easy to figure out. Our jobs as husbands, is to seek to understand how they *feel*, and sometimes not even provide solutions. Sometimes, they just want to be heard," The Icon said.

"You mean they don't want us to solve the problem? What good is that?" I questioned.

"Vincent, there are some things that us men will never understand about women," The Icon said chuckling to himself.

"I don't understand. When I have problems, I want solutions!" I said.

"You may think you do, however stop and really think through this, Vincent. *Rule Number Nineteen* applies to men too. You may think you want solutions, and maybe you do, but you also want to be *heard*. It's a human desire to be heard and understood. People want their feelings to be validated, men and women alike," said The Icon.

I guess I never really thought of it that way. The Icon was right. One of the most memorable experiences I had with him was when he invited me over to his home for dinner when my dad had nothing but negative things to say about my internship.

He and Isabella *listened*.

They *heard* me.

They shared their experiences with me, but they never told me what to do. They never gave me *advice*.

That was what the next rule, *Rule Number Twenty*, was all about.

"Vincent, giving someone the answer to their problem rarely ever works. That's why I don't like giving *advice*. If you really want to help someone make a good decision, it's better to help people clarify their options about how to handle their situation, and let them come to their own decision. This allows them to take ownership over developing their own solution and plan of attack. It also holds them accountable to their outcome. *Rule Number Twenty: Empower people to make their own decisions*," The Icon said.

He continued, "People love to blame other people for their outcomes, and so it's wiser to help people come to their own decisions, based on what's most important to them. Because if you push them too hard to make the decision that YOU think they should, and for whatever reason, it doesn't work out, who do you think they're going to blame?"

"They're gonna blame me," I said.

"Exactly. I've seen good intentions destroy relationships because of this. Let people talk their way through their situation and their potential solutions. It's always better to ask them questions than it is to be an advice-giver. Once a person hears themselves say what's most important to them, they'll most often make a decision that's in line with their priorities."

"But what if their priorities are all messed up?" I questioned.

"Messed up by who's standards? Yours? Vincent, everyone's got their own standards. They've got their own priorities. If their priorities aren't in line with yours, who are you to judge?" The Icon stated.

I immediately thought about the conversation I had with Lindsey, Joseph's assistant.

"Vincent, you've got to let people make their own mistakes sometimes. Just empower them to make their own decisions, and help them see all the angles and potential outcomes. What you'll find is that if you do this right, they'll ultimately make the best decision for THEM," The Icon confidently said.

I promised myself that I would one day master The Icon's life rules. However, there were three more rules that he would share with me before the evening was over.

"Vincent, do you think I'm a great leader?" The Icon asked.

"Sir, you're the best. You know that," I said.

"And what makes me a great leader? Really think about this one Vincent. What makes you think I'm a great leader?" The Icon prodded.

"Well, you certainly have the greatest following. People continuously say they owe their life to you," I responded.

"Personally, I think they're giving me way too much credit, but think about what you said. People feel like they owe their lives to me. Why is that? I'll tell you why. It's because my entire life has been about serving other people," The Icon explained.

"You see, people have followed me in business because I've listened with the intention of understanding, and because they all know that I lead with a *Servant Leadership* mentality. *Rule Number Twenty-One: The greatest leader is the greatest servant.*" The Icon explained.

I hung on The Icon's every word.

Golden nugget after golden nugget left his lips, as he explained in great detail what he believed in.

Living by this set of rules and teaching them to others so that they might live a life of greatness was The Icon's main mission in life.

"Another reason I've had a strong following is that everyone knows that I've always put our team above myself. There's a whole lot of so-called leaders out there that take their people to the mountain top, put their arm around them and essentially say, '*If you work really hard... and really commit yourself to me... ALL of this can be MINE.*' They don't actually say that, but that's how they make their people feel. If you want to build an army of soldiers, you've got to make people feel that you will always put the team above self. Everything must be for the greater good of the team. As a leader, your people will follow you if and only if they feel that you put the team first. The minute they start feeling like your intentions are selfish and self-serving, they'll turn against you. *Rule Number Twenty-Two: Put the team above self,*" The Icon explained.

This was the way The Icon lived his life.

He made everyone feel important.

No one ever accused The Icon of being selfish.

If anything, he developed a reputation of being overly generous.

It's amazing that more people don't get that.

The more you give, the more you get. Those people that hoard everything for themselves often end up with nothing.

Then The Icon said something that made my ears perk up more than ever.

"Vincent, this may be the most important rule that I'm about to share with you right now, specifically for you. *Rule Number Twenty-Three: Forgiveness is for the forgiver.* Vincent, I know your relationship with your dad has been strained for many years, as was mine. But you see, I never took the chance to forgive my dad before he died. I spent so many years resenting my father for not being the father I wanted him to be. I held a grudge for the longest time. When I finally forgave my dad, it was too late for him to reap the benefit. But forgiveness is not for the *forgiven*. The real gift of forgiveness is for the *forgiver*," The Icon explained.

My eyes slowly began to fill up with tears.

"You see Vincent, when you forgive someone, you're not acknowledging their actions as being acceptable. What you're really doing is acknowledging that as hurtful as their actions or words may have been, you're making a decision to move on with your life, freeing yourself from the shackles of resentment. You see, resentment holds you back in life. When you hold on to resentment, it continues to occupy a space in your heart. But when you let it go, that space frees itself up to be filled with something positive... something wonderful. Once you make the decision to move on and achieve greatness in spite of what someone else said or did to you, you become free, and that freedom is what allows happiness to follow. And so when you forgive someone, ultimately, it isn't for *their* benefit. It's for *your own* benefit," The Icon said.

Once again, as The Icon taught me one of his sacred rules, he concurrently put into practice another one of his rules.

Rule Number Twenty was to empower people to make their own decisions, and here was The Icon, teaching me about forgiveness, while at the same time not telling me what to do regarding my relationship with my father.

He always taught me these valuable lessons through stories of his own personal experiences. He never held anything back regarding sharing mistakes he's made in the past, which made him relatable, even as great of a man as he was.

In fact, that's what made him even greater.

He was the first one to tell you that he wasn't perfect.

He had bulletproof confidence, yet he was also humble at the same time. That was the balance of extremes that I aspired to achieve.

"Sir, you've taught me twenty-three rules so far. How many rules are there in total?" I humbly asked.

The Icon smiled at me, admiring my curiosity and my insatiable appetite for learning. He knew how much I looked up to him, and how much I aspired to embody the level of greatness that he lived by.

"Vincent, every lesson – every rule – shall be revealed in due time, as there is a *right time* for certain lessons to be revealed. I've tried my entire life to figure it out – to rush the process – and I've found that if you're constantly searching for the answers to better yourself as a person, the lessons will be revealed when they are supposed to be revealed. There are twenty-four rules in total, and I trust that the twenty-forth rule shall be revealed to you when it is time," The Icon said.

Spiritual discernment was one of many gifts that The Icon had in his arsenal of amazing qualities.

He was so wise – not just smart – but *wise*.

I believe it was his faith in the universal truths of his rules that allowed The Icon to operate with such certainty.

He had laid down the blueprint for so many of us – the blueprint of how to live a successful life, both in our personal lives as well as in our business lives. He was able to simplify life's most complex and puzzling issues, and distill them down into a format that gave people clarity.

Living by his set of rules made life seem almost *easy*.

Sure, sometimes bad things happen to good people, and sure, we're all faced with many challenges in our lives, but *living right* as The Icon put it, allows us the possibility of turning obstacles into opportunities – mayhem into miracles.

I remember The Icon telling me that life is a lot like a slingshot. With a slingshot, the further you pull it back, the further it shoots the rock forward. He explained to me that sometimes God pulls you back further because His intention is to slingshot you further ahead – beyond what you could have ever dreamed of yourself. Sometimes, you have to take a step backwards in order to take two steps forwards.

I thought about Andrei pocketing half-eaten leftovers off customers' plates at his coffee shop job and eating them for dinner.

I thought about what Joseph and Christine went through in their first year of marriage, eating *Top Ramen* for dinner, struggling to pay their bills.

I thought about Isabella's experience of escaping her family's criminal associations, and her journey from Columbia to New York.

I thought about Francisco's parents being murdered, and his journey from Nicaragua to Beverly Hills.

And I thought about my divorce and my father's lack of support, and how these seemingly negative experiences were all part of my journey from a life of mediocrity to a life of ultimate fulfillment.

Each one of these challenges and adversities wasn't so much a *set back*, but rather a *set up*. Each one of these *less-than-perfect* situations created an opportunity for something great to happen.

Had The Icon never seen Andrei pocket the scraps of food, he wouldn't have stopped him in the parking lot, and perhaps Andrei would have never been afforded the opportunity to have a mentor like The Icon.

If Joseph hadn't struggled in his first year at the firm, perhaps Christine wouldn't have been afforded the opportunity to prove how much she believed in her husband. Had that not happened, perhaps their bond and their marriage wouldn't be what it is today.

If Isabella hadn't experienced her family's corruption in Columbia, perhaps she wouldn't have made the decision to escape and move to New York, in which case, she would have never met The Icon, and Valentina would have never been born.

If Francisco hadn't been busted selling necklaces and bracelets to tourists at the resort in Nicaragua, perhaps he would have never crossed paths with The Icon, and his brothers wouldn't have become attorneys, his sister a CPA, and he an equity partner in the hottest hotel in Beverly Hills.

And if I hadn't gone through a divorce, I would have never been afforded the opportunity to marry Valentina.

It sounded crazy to hear myself think those thoughts.

Something that I thought was the *worst* thing that could have ever happened to me – having my ex-wife leave me – ended up being the *best* thing that ever happened to me.

The Icon believed that all of these outcomes were destined to happen – divinely designed plans that were engineered from the very beginning.

Everything, The Icon believed, was a *set up*.

The Icon believed that God allowed us to go through trials and adversities in order to see if we were worthy of the magnificent blessings He planned on bestowing upon us, and that every tribulation was used to prepare us for a miracle.

This was the concept of the slingshot... to be pulled backwards in order to be slingshotted into the stars.

Andrei, Joseph, Francisco, Isabella, Valentina and I were all recipients of a miracle. We had all been touched by The Icon, a man whose commitment to impact other people's lives was a personal mission. We were all eternally grateful to have had the opportunity to walk with such a man.

The next six weeks would be six excruciatingly painful weeks for The Icon, but he remained an inspiration to everyone all the way up until the very end.

On The Icon's final evening, he laid in his hospital bed, smiling at Isabella, Valentina and me.

It was time.

"Isabella," he said. "You have made my life complete. You've been my co-pilot in life, and have taught me the most important lessons I know. Because of you, I've laughed harder... I've loved deeper... and I've enjoyed smelling the roses along the way. Without you, all of my success would have meant nothing. Thank you for believing in me all these years. Thank you for loving me all these years. You have made me the luckiest man alive."

The Icon's love and devotion to Isabella was never questioned by anyone, yet in that moment, I was able to see into his heart in a way that I had never seen before.

He was so grateful for his life, and for his co-pilot.

He had travelled the world, holding Isabella's hand the entire way. It was a relationship that was truly inspiring.

The Icon then said, "Valentina, sweetheart. I'm so proud of you. Your entire life, you've been a champion. I remember when you first told me that you wanted to be an entrepreneur. Part of me was so excited, and yet the other part of me worried that you wanted this because you thought that I wanted this for you. I feared that you wanted to please me so badly that you would do it at the expense of your own happiness. But I see now that you were born to do this. You were born with the entrepreneur gene. I'm so proud of everything you've accomplished. Just know that as proud of you as I am today, what made me the most proud was when you had the guts to start your first store, taking out those high-interest bank loans. Above and beyond your results, I've always been proud of you for your guts and for your effort. You did it all on your own, without any of my help, and you should be proud of that."

"But papa, I didn't do any of this on my own. You've taught me everything I know about business. You've been my mentor ever since I was a little girl. You and mama have always believed in me. My confidence comes from the both of you.

Papa, thank you for giving me the life you've given me. Thank you for working so hard when you were young and single, before you ever met mama. Without your vision, I would have never been able to..." Valentina said, unable to finish her sentence as she began sobbing uncontrollably.

Valentina knew it was time to say goodbye.

Sometimes there are no words that seem appropriate for the situation. Sometimes all you can do is hold their hand, run your fingers through their hair, and kiss them on the cheek... and perhaps that's better than any words could ever articulate your love for them.

Then The Icon asked me to put my head next to his, sharing his pillow with me. I kissed him on the forehead, and put my hand on his shoulder, as he had done so many times with me.

He and I had shared so many wonderful conversations together over the years, and many intense ones over the last six weeks. We had shared how much we meant to each other, and so there was nothing that wasn't said that needed to be said. I would treasure every conversation I'd ever had with The Icon – my mentor.

As I laid next to him – two grown men, sharing a pillow together – The Icon whispered in my ear, "Vincent, you're going to be the man of our family now. Promise me you'll take care of my girls."

As tears trickled down my cheeks onto his, I squeezed his hand and nodded my head in confirmation... and once he received my confirmation – a confirmation he knew that I would commit my life to – he said his final goodbye.

Chapter Eighteen
The 24ᵗʰ Rule

One year after The Icon had passed, I found myself feeling so many mixed emotions.

I missed my mentor.

I missed my friend.

Yet his absence made me appreciate him and everything he'd done for me that much more.

The thing about The Icon's effect on my life was that his lessons never stopped guiding me. He had given me twenty-three rules to live by, and these rules – the rules that he'd taught Andrei, Joseph, Francisco and me – laid down the blueprint of how to live a successful life, not only in business, but in all areas of our lives.

My relationship with Valentina had deepened, no doubt as a result of applying these same rules to our marriage. And she, being The Icon's daughter, knew all of them as well.

He had taught her everything he knew, and his mentorship, along with Isabella's influence as her mother, made Valentina one-in-a-million.

We visited Isabella quite often, sometimes out on the West Coast, and sometimes flying her out to New York. On one trip to LA, during a quiet dinner at Isabella's home, she gave me a gift that felt like The Icon was teaching me from the grave.

She asked me to follow her from the dining room into The Icon's home office.

On the wall, hung a framed quote that said,

When a tiger dies, he leaves behind his skin.

When an elephant dies, he leaves behind his tusks.

And when a man dies, he leaves behind his name.

The quote was handwritten, and framed in an odd frame that looked like a little kid had painted it. Isabella looked at the oddly framed quote with these wise words that embodied everything The Icon lived for.

She smiled and said, "This was a gift that Francisco gave my husband when they first moved back here from Nicaragua, when Francisco was only 18-years old. It was an old saying that his parents had taught him when he was a child, and even at the tender age of eighteen, Francisco understood the impact that my husband had made on his family. Of all my husband's possessions, this gift was his most prized possession."

The Icon had left behind a name to be proud of.

He had truly left behind a legacy.

Isabella reached up, removed the framed quote from the wall, and said, "Vincent, Papa would have wanted you to have this."

She handed it to me, and instantly, it became *my* most prized possession.

As I held this work of art in my hands – something that held so much history and sentiment to my mentor – Isabella looked at me and said, "Vincent, this is *Rule Number Twenty-Four: When a man dies, he leaves behind his name.*"

I remember in one of my last conversations with The Icon, he told me that the *rules* would be revealed to me in due time.

I found it ironic that the final rule – *Rule Number Twenty-Four* – would be revealed after The Icon's passing. But when I thought about how The Icon lived his life, it wasn't ironic at all.

It was textbook perfect.

He believed that the *rules* weren't *his rules* per say, but rather rules that came from a higher power. He believed that this set of rules was greater than him, that these rules would transcend time. He believed that even in his physical absence, that the rules would continue to teach those that aspired to become great.

This beautiful life lesson that an 18-year old Francisco passed on to The Icon would now hang on the wall in my bathroom, right next to my sink where I brushed my teeth every morning.

I wanted to start off everyday reading it as I brushed my teeth, to remind me what life was all about.

Our interior designer said it didn't go with the décor of our bathroom, but I didn't care. I wanted it to be a constant reminder of how I wanted to live my life.

I wanted to be able to impact other people's lives the way The Icon did, and leave behind a name that my future kids could be proud of.

This gift that hung on my bathroom wall would inspire me to write a *Success Manual* for my unborn children, containing all the life applicable rules that The Icon had taught me.

Valentina was now two months pregnant with our first son, Cortez, and I wanted to make sure that in the event of my untimely death, that he would have this set of life lessons in an organized manuscript to guide him through his life.

I wanted, as The Icon had done for me, to be able to teach my son from the grave.

I took a trip to San Juan del Sur, Nicaragua with Valentina, the same city where the 15-year old Francisco had met The Icon, to begin constructing the framework of my *Success Manual*.

I figured it would be good to *get away* and begin writing the manuscript in a quiet environment – an environment where I could be inspired to create something great.

We arrived in Managua – Nicaragua's capital city – at the *Managua Sandino Airport*. A nice man named Armando picked us up in a private car to transport us to San Juan del Sur, about an hour and a half drive from the airport.

Once in San Juan del Sur, we rented a 4x4 SUV to drive to our accommodations. Valentina searched online for private vacation residences, and found a private home in a community of eleven homes nestled up in the mountains above San Juan del Sur, something we thought would be better than staying in a standard hotel in town.

The community was called *Los Balcónes*.

It was an obscure 25-minute journey from town to our mystery residence. I knew we were in for an adventure when we made a left-hand turn off the main road onto a dirt road, and put our SUV into 4-wheel drive mode. The dirt road wove through a small little village, something similar to what I envisioned Francisco growing up in.

And though I didn't see Francisco's actual home, I saw many small shacks along the dirt road as we drove from the town to our very fortunate accommodations up in the hills. I saw the cinder block constructed homes that Francisco had talked about with the corrugated sheet metal roofs.

Those were the *nicer* homes.

Many of the other homes were made of scrap wood frames with makeshift walls, jury-rigged together with several plastic bags held together with duct tape. Many of these makeshift homes had dirt floors and no doors.

It was humbling to see that kind of poverty.

To think that Francisco – a multi-millionaire today – came from such humble beginnings. To think that The Icon could see the potential in a 15-year old boy. To think that he adopted Francisco's siblings so that they could come to the United States to pursue *The American Dream* together.

Again, it was very humbling to let these thoughts sink into your soul, realizing the magnitude of The Icon's vision about what was possible.

We then made another left-hand turn onto a smaller dirt road, entering the jungle. This road was full of deep potholes, making our ride feel like we were riding a bucking bronco.

As we navigated through this tropical rainforest, I admired the beauty, but questioned the safety.

We had no idea what our Nicaraguan adventure had in store for us.

I knew that we had arrived at our destination when we saw a giant hand-carved wooden sign that read *Los Balcónes*. The guard at the front gate greeted us with a warm smile.

Fortunately, Valentina's Spanish speaking abilities allowed us to communicate with the guard, who as I found out later, stood at his post all day in the hot Nicaraguan sun, guarding the entrance to our house in the hills.

I put our SUV into first gear and began climbing the steep, winding dirt and rock road that supposedly led to our home at the top of the mountain. The road was just wide enough for our SUV, with no walking room on either side.

The guard told us to *hug* the right side of the road, because the left side fell straight off a cliff into oblivion. Driving on this skinny, bumpy road made me a bit nervous, to say the least.

I guess they didn't believe in guardrails in Nicaragua.

But when we reached the top of the mountain, the view was so breathtaking that my hyperventilating subsided.

Our home was called *Casa de Mono*. You know a home is cool when it has its own name.

The English translation of *Casa de Mono* was *House of the Monkey*. At first, I thought it was an odd name for a home, but as I would later discover, there were magnificent, friendly Nicaraguan monkeys that lived in the trees surrounding the home. We were literally *in the jungle*.

Valentina walked into the home first, as I unloaded our SUV, grabbing our luggage.

"Vincent, come look! Hurry!" Valentina exclaimed.

I dropped our luggage immediately, and ran inside.

The home was amazing.

The entrance to the property had a large teak wooden door that led into the main living space – a huge, covered outdoor courtyard with an incredible outdoor kitchen. The ceilings were artfully crafted in bamboo, and giant ceiling fans gently cooled the pavilionesque outdoor living space.

I briefly sat down on one of the white pillow-covered chaise lounges next to the infinity pool, and as I gazed out over the panoramic ocean view, I thought to myself, "This is why I worked so hard. Thank God I didn't quit."

The bedrooms were located in a separate structure off to the left, beautifully finished with teak wood throughout. The home was both modern and rustic at the same time. The architectural lines of the home were very clean and minimalist, yet the teak wood gave it a warm, tropical feel.

There were two large master bedrooms, identical to each other, with giant sliding teak doors on one side that opened up into the courtyard, giving us an indoor/outdoor feel.

On the other side of each bedroom were beautiful French doors that opened up onto private balconies with panoramic views of the ocean, the mountains, and the jungle.

We said hello to a few friendly *monos* – Nicaragua monkeys – that swung from the trees keeping us company.

The name of this exclusive, private development said it all. *Los Balcónes*, which translated into English, meant *The Balconies*. Practically every room and every living space in *Casa de Mono* had a panoramic view, like you were literally living on a massive ocean view balcony, in the middle of the jungle.

There was a level of tranquility that was perfect for me to start writing my manuscript.

Valentina and I stayed in our *Balcony In The Sky* home for two weeks while I worked on the manuscript containing the twenty-four rules.

I would wake up early in the morning, run down the hill to a great little surf spot called *Madéras* and catch some killer waves. After a fun surf session, I'd drive into town and pick up some locally caught fresh fish – dorado, langosta, and whatever else the catch-of-the-day happened to be.

We'd grill the locally caught seafood in our outdoor kitchen that overlooked the infinity pool and our magnificent panoramic view of *San Juan del Sur*.

There was a wonderful artisan bakery in town called *Pan de Vida* that had delicious cinnamon rolls and Nicaraguan *pan dulce*, a Latin sweet bread that had way too many carbs for one human being to ingest, but I joyfully ate them anyway.

I was never a big drinker, however I did learn to enjoy a nice sipping tequila from time to time. But while in Nicaragua, I traded in my *Frida Kahlo añejo* for some dark, aged *Flor de Caña*, a locally produced Nicaraguan rum.

Everyday we ate freshly picked dragon fruit, pineapples, papayas, and plantains – all locally grown – as well as fresh, locally caught fish. I must admit, there was something *cleansing* about living a simple, stripped-down life while on vacation. Everyday, I'd wear surf trunks, sandals, and no shirt.

I even grew a goatee.

We'd sit in the infinity pool, staring off through the beautiful jungle foliage out to the ocean, as a perfect combination of the warm Nicaraguan sun and the pleasant *Balcónes* mountain breeze massaged our souls. Valentina and I would watch the sunset from our mountaintop view every night, holding each other's hand, and marveling at what our lives had become.

We would talk about The Icon, and our many experiences with him – a brilliant mentor to me, and a wonderful father to Valentina.

From time to time, I would become overwhelmed with sadness as I thought about how much I missed him. But that's not how The Icon would have wanted me to remember him, and so I focused on celebrating the time that I did have with him, and I did my very best to perpetuate his legacy.

After Valentina would go to sleep, I'd stay up several hours, writing down everything The Icon had ever taught me… every lesson… every rule. The manuscript started to come together, as if The Icon's spirit was present, guiding me through every detail of every life lesson he had taught me over the years.

Each rule he had taught me came to life all over again as I wrote them out. It was a cathartic experience for me, reliving each moment that either Andrei, Joseph or The Icon himself had spent time with me to explain this set of *life rules* – a set of rules that would not only become a blueprint of how I would live my own life, but one that I could pass on to my kids, and they could pass on to theirs.

Fourteen days later, I had finished the framework of my manuscript. I came to realize that constructing this manuscript was one of the many ways I could memorialize The Icon's life. It was how my unborn son would learn about his grandfather and the impact he made on not only my life, but on the rest of the world.

I would name my son *Cortez*, after the Spanish Conquistador that had told his men to *Burn The Ships*, and I would make sure that he understood *Rule Number Eleven*.

And so the manuscript explained The Icon's twenty-four rules, describing each rule in great detail, including its application to living a successful life, as The Icon had done for me.

This was The Icon's legacy.

On the last evening of our Nicaraguan adventure, just before sunset, we stopped by *El Cien* to have dinner, and although it was under different management, The Icon had definitely left his mark.

It was a spectacular property.

As I walked through the magnificent resort, I realized that The Icon had built his Bel Air home as a near perfect replica of *El Cien*.

Seeing where The Icon started his business empire was nothing short of a historic and iconic experience for me.

I envisioned The Icon at 31-years old, working day and night, weekdays and weekends, non-stop... with a 15-year old Francisco trailing him, absorbing everything The Icon had to teach him.

I thought about the two of them grinding it out non-stop, from sun-up to sun-down, and well into the night, building what would eventually become the cornerstone of their success – a mentor/mentee partnership that started out as one benevolent soul deciding to help out a poor Nicaraguan kid, giving him a job.

This was the mentor/mentee relationship that each one of The Icon's businesses was based on.

Never in my wildest dreams did I ever think that The Icon would envision me running one of his companies, let alone becoming a partner, and eventually inheriting part of his legacy.

I don't think Andrei or Joseph had such visions of grandeur either, at least not to the level that The Icon raised them to achieve. And certainly the 15-year old Francisco, living in a small Nicaraguan village, sleeping on a concrete floor, doing his best to take care of his younger siblings all by himself, would never aspire to, nor dream about living the life he had built for himself.

I guess that's where faith comes in.

It's the belief that *anything* is possible… that if you do what's right… if you work relentlessly on improving yourself as a person… and if you're fortunate enough to be blessed with a great mentor… that dreams can come true – dreams that far surpass anything that you could have fathomed on your own.

The Icon saw me not for my *past*, but for my *possibilities*. He didn't focus on my *imperfections*, but rather my *improvements*. He taught me how to turn my *setbacks* into *set-ups* for success.

The Icon was my hero, and I hoped that one day, I would be able to impact other people's lives the way he impacted mine.

Chapter Nineteen
Picking Up The Torch

I came back from Nicaragua with The Icon's lessons organized in a completed manuscript.

I called it *The Icon Effect: 24 Essential Rules Of Success*.

Once it was completed, it made me appreciate even more just how much these rules had changed my life.

I never really thought of myself as an author, but I self-published the manuscript and started handing it out to my friends – people that I cared about that I wanted to reap the same benefits from these rules that I had been taught.

The response I got was overwhelming.

Then I gave a copy to everyone at my firm... everyone at Joseph's firm... everyone at Andrei's firm... and every single employee at *Madre's*.

Valentina recommended that I work on turning the manuscript into a full-fledged book, writing an autobiography about my rise to success, and how I learned each of these rules from my mentors.

She always believed in my vision.

She always believed in *me*.

That's the thing about having the right co-pilot. When your co-pilot can see potential in you that even surpasses your own visions of grandeur, you know you're with the right co-pilot.

It reminded me of a conversation I had years ago, right after my divorce. I was having dinner with a dear friend of mine, Thomas.

I was pouring my heart out to him about how devastated I was about my divorce, and how I had felt like I was such a failure in life. I shared with him how so many people had criticized me for never living up to their expectations, and how I was nothing compared to my brother Derek.

My friend Thomas had a great sense of humor. He said, "Vincent, close your eyes. Don't worry dude, I'm not going to touch you or anything."

We both started laughing, which lightened up the mood temporarily. But then it immediately got serious again.

He said, "Seriously Vincent, close your eyes. I want you to think about everyone in your life that has ever criticized you. Think about all the people that never believed in you. Think about all the people that told you that you weren't good enough... that made you feel like you were a failure... that made you feel like you didn't measure up."

As I thought about all of these people – my dad... my ex-wife... former baseball coaches... ex-bosses... etc. – I became seethingly angry. I sat there with my eyes closed, clenching my teeth.

The rage and resentment began to build within me like the steam within a pressure cooker, ready to explode.

But then Thomas said something that changed my emotional state on a dime.

He said, "As you think about all of these people that have hurt you, think about how they see you."

Thomas paused for a few seconds as I dwelled on this disempowering moment, and then he said, "And as you think about how all of these people see you, now think about how God sees you."

Tears began to stream down my face.

Thomas said, "Vincent, I know it's painful to think about the hurtful things that all of those people have said to you in your life. There's nothing more painful than the feeling of unacceptance. But God loves you. He made you. He made you with all of your great qualities, as well as your imperfections. Do you know what that means? It means that He never expected you to be perfect, and even with all of your imperfections, he still loves you. He still accepts you. Maybe your dad and your ex-wife didn't... but He does. One day, you'll find an amazing girl that's deserving of the wonderful man you are, and she'll see a level of greatness inside of you that maybe you don't even see yourself. She'll see you the way God sees you."

Thomas was such a great friend to me back then.

We had gone our separate ways in life, as he had moved to Spain to pursue his career in the culinary arts, but we had kept in touch via email over the years.

Thomas was a beautiful soul.

He reminded me, in many ways, of Francisco. He was one of those people that warmed up a room just by walking into it.

As I reminisced over Thomas's wise words he'd shared with me years ago, in that moment, I realized that his words had come to pass.

God had blessed me with a wife that saw me the way He saw me. Valentina could see possibilities within me that I couldn't even see within myself.

Even at this point in my life, with all that I had achieved, Valentina believed that I was just getting started. It's amazing what having the right woman in your life can do for you.

Just as The Icon was the wind beneath my wings in my development as a man, Valentina provided the wind I needed to evolve into a great husband, and eventually, a great father.

For the next year, I would wake up a couple of hours before Valentina and our son Cortez, and I would write. I'd be in our living room, writing in the dark before the sun came up, developing the architecture of my book. I didn't want to sacrifice family time, and I sure as heck didn't want to sacrifice my primary business of running the firm. Giving up a few hours of sleep seemed like a prudent thing to do in an effort to work on this project.

Similar to my West Coast days of surfing, I found great pleasure in waking up and accomplishing something before the rest of the world got out of bed.

There was always something very satisfying about that.

Once the first draft copy was completed, I had Joseph and his wife Christine read it.

I had Andrei read it.

I had Isabella read it.

And of course, I had Valentina read it.

It was my life, out there on full display for the world to see. I recounted all of my experiences, all of my mistakes, and all of my emotions throughout the process of learning *the rules*.

It was the most vulnerable I had ever felt.

All of my innermost feelings were explained in great detail for the world to judge – all of my screw-ups and humbling experiences on display for other people to scrutinize.

But as my dear old friend Thomas taught me way back when, the only real opinion of me that mattered was God's.

What I had grown to realize was that the people that were closest to me – The Icon, Isabella, Joseph, Andrei and Valentina – they all saw me the way God saw me.

They all loved me and accepted me, despite all of my flaws. They never judged me for my *past*, but rather celebrated me for my *future*.

In the process of finishing the final draft of my book, I humbly decided to add a twenty-fifth rule to The Icon's set of rules. *Rule Number Twenty-Five: Never forget how God sees you.*

When Valentina told me that my manuscript-turned-autobiography was going to be bigger than life, I had no idea how right she was.

After I found a literary agent to represent my book, I had a book deal within a year.

With my book deal, came speaking events.

With speaking events, came media exposure.

I was reluctant to move forward with my motivational speaking career because I didn't want it to distract me from building the firm's New York office, but Joseph encouraged me to move forward with it. He said it would be great PR for the firm, giving us national exposure.

Boy, was he right.

I became somewhat of a celebrity in the financial industry as a result of *The Icon Effect*. The exposure that my motivational talks and book sales gave me provided a platform for me to promote my firm.

And due to this massive exposure, we now had investment brokers, financial advisors, and insurance agents BEGGING us to join our firm.

We tripled the size of the New York office in less than a year, and the LA office doubled as well.

Book sales were up. Never in my wildest dreams would I have thought I'd be an acclaimed author.

I was now giving keynote speeches at national industry events. But nothing gave me more joy than giving talks to high school students about my rise to success. I wanted them to know that they too could achieve greatness.

My message was, essentially, that if I could do it... then they could do it too.

And it wasn't just the firm that was doing well.

Our entire crew was crushing it.

Madre's Coffee was now an international brand. Valentina had brilliantly grown the brand organically in the beginning, but now we were growing exponentially.

When Valentina and I decided to have our second child, we decided it was time to sell.

We took *Madre's* public, and walked away with more money than we could ever spend in one lifetime.

Andrei's jewelry company was on fire now more than ever too, and he had inherited The Icon's luxury men's clothing company. He and Massimo outfitted my entire wardrobe. Andrei's brand was being worn by every A-List celebrity, and had expanded beyond his *Made-To-Measure* bespoke line.

He now had an entire *Ready-To-Wear* line that was being carried at Barney's, Neiman Marcus, and his own boutique stores all over the world.

The firm was making headlines right and left. Joseph and I had opened additional offices in Chicago, Dallas, Miami and we were contemplating London.

We were at the top of our game, and even had our own hedge fund that was collecting an asset pool bigger than life itself.

Whenever I was in LA, I would always make it a point to stop by the *Madre's* location where I had first met Valentina and The Icon, mostly to reminisce about *The Good Ole Days.*

Obviously, when I was at home in New York, I would frequent the *Madre's* location where I had been reunited with Valentina.

They still made the best Americano around.

On my most recent trip to LA, I made my routine stop at *Madre's*. As I sat down to enjoy my Grande Americano, with three Splendas, a dash of cream, and an extra shot of Espresso, a young man in his mid-twenties was eyeballing me from a table in the corner.

After about ten minutes of scoping me out, he stood up and approached my table.

He said, "Excuse me sir, is that an *IWC DaVinci – Kurt Klaus Edition?*" as he pointed to my watch.

The Icon had left this watch to me in his will.

It was my favorite watch, one, because it held sentimental value due to the fact that it was The Icon's favorite watch... and two, it was also the watch he wore the first time I had ever met him.

"Yes it is," I replied.

"Wow!" he said. "Rose gold ones like that are hard to come by."

"You're clearly into watches I see," I said, impressed that a young kid would know about this particular watch and its rarity.

"Yeah, well, I'm a watch dealer... sort of," he said, avoiding eye contact.

I could tell he was shy about his career, and perhaps even a bit self-conscious about his lack of success. I knew that look, because it was the same look I used to have before I had met The Icon.

This kid seemed driven, enthusiastic and passionate, but I could tell his focus was scattered. We talked for a good thirty minutes. He asked me a million and one questions about what I did, and how I became successful.

He told me about his watch dealing business and the dismal success he'd had thus far.

I sensed his frustration. It reminded me of how I felt back when I had first met The Icon. And then it dawned on me.

Back when The Icon had made his offer to mentor me, I had asked him why he was willing to help me, and he told me that I reminded him of someone.

In that moment, I realized the person I reminded him of, was himself.

Driven people can spot another driven person from a mile away. It's something in their energy... in their spirit. There's an aura they give off, and it doesn't matter if they're an aspiring entrepreneur, or one that has already made millions. We all have one main thing in common.

We all have a dream.

"What's your name, son?" I asked.

"Kane," he replied.

"Kane. That's an interesting name," I said.

"Yeah, my parents are from Ireland. They came to the states when I was only 3-years old. In Gaelic, *Kane* means 'battler' which is what I am," he explained.

That made me like this kid even more.

He was hungry.

He was scrappy.

He was just like me when I first met The Icon.

At the end of our conversation, Kane was so appreciative of the fact that I had given him so much of my time. It was a quality that I deeply admired – a heart of *appreciation*.

As I finished my Americano, I stood up to shake his hand.

And as he asked me for my business card, I said, "I don't have any cards on me at the moment, but I've got something better than that."

Shocked, the young man looked at me and said, "Huh?"

I smiled and told him that he reminded me of someone I once knew.

"Oh yeah? Who's that?" he inquired.

I responded, "Perhaps I'll tell you one day. But for right now, I've got seven words for you, kid."

1. Meet
2. Me
3. Here
4. Tomorrow
5. Morning
6. At
7. 8:00 AM

The 25 Rules

Rule #1a: Don't Ever Be Late.

Rule #1b: If You're Not At Least 15 Minutes Early, Then You're Late.

Rule #2: Don't Ever Let Your Brain Be Lazy.

Rule #3: If You Want What Average People Have, Do What They Do.

Rule #4: Seek Different Perspectives, But Never Ask For Advice.

Rule #5: The Greatest Pleasure In Life Is Accomplishing Things Other People Said You Could Not Do.

Rule #6: Accepting Help Doesn't Make You Any Less Of A Man.

Rule #7: Never Sell Yourself Short.

Rule #8: Your Beginning Days Of Struggle Will One Day Be Your *Good Ole Days.*

Rule #9: Never Despise The Days Of Small Beginnings.

Rule #10: Never Blame Others.

Rule #11: Burn Your Ships.

Rule #12: Erase The Word *Should* From Your Vocabulary.

Rule #13: Never Judge Another Person's Drive.

Rule #14: Whoever Is Willing To Walk Away First, Has The Power.

Rule #15: Don't Try To *Find* The Right Person. Just Focus On *Being* The Right Person.

Rule #16: It's You And Your Spouse Against The World.

Rule #17: You Don't Have To *Know*. You Just Have To *Believe*.

Rule #18: Be Thankful For What You Have, While You Work For What You Want.

Rule #19: Listen To *Understand*, Not To *Respond*.

Rule #20: Empower People To Make Their Own Decisions.

Rule #21: The Greatest Leader Is The Greatest Servant.

Rule #22: Put The Team Above Self.

Rule #23: Forgiveness Is For The Forgiver.

Rule #24: When A Man Dies, He Leaves Behind His Name.

Rule #25: Never Forget How God Sees You.

About The Author

Darren Sugiyama is a successful entrepreneur who has built several successful companies in multiple industries.

As a business development consultant, Darren has been sought out by multi-million dollar and billion dollar corporations, seeking his advice on marketing, branding, and leadership strategies.

Today, Darren is a nationally recognized motivational speaker, inspiring entrepreneurs all over the country, and is also an acclaimed author.

His first book, ***How I Built a $37 Million Dollar Insurance Agency In Less Than 7 Years*** has gained national recognition, and is the insurance industry's most cutting edge book, in which Darren shares his secrets on how he built his insurance empire, from nothing.

In his second book, ***Living Outside The Cubicle – The Ultimate Success Guide For The Aspiring Entrepreneur***, Darren reveals his philosophies about living a successful life.

His third book, ***The 6-Figure Retirement – The Best Kept Secret On How To Retire Wealthy***, is takes an unapologetically blunt angle at explaining the world of life insurance, investments, and wealth management.

Darren also hosts business development and sales coaching *Boot Camp Seminars* where entrepreneurs and sales executives from all over the country fly into Orange County, California and learn from Darren himself.

Despite Darren's busy schedule, he still finds time to give back to the community, talking with and encouraging young people to think about their life choices and their future careers. He has done several speaking engagements at various universities, high schools and middle schools.

For more information about Darren Sugiyama, visit his website at **www.DarrenSugiyama.com**.